Mapping
The Cultures
of the West

✳ ✳ ✳

Mapping
The Cultures
of the West

VOLUME 1: *to* 1750

CLIFFORD R. BACKMAN
Boston University

New York   Oxford
OXFORD UNIVERSITY PRESS

Oxford University Press is a department of the University of Oxford.
It furthers the University's objective of excellence in research,
scholarship, and education by publishing worldwide.

Oxford New York
Auckland Cape Town Dar es Salaam Hong Kong Karachi
Kuala Lumpur Madrid Melbourne Mexico City Nairobi
New Delhi Shanghai Taipei Toronto

With offices in
Argentina Austria Brazil Chile Czech Republic France Greece
Guatemala Hungary Italy Japan Poland Portugal Singapore
South Korea Switzerland Thailand Turkey Ukraine Vietnam

Copyright © 2014 by Oxford University Press

For titles covered by Section 112 of the US Higher Education
Opportunity Act, please visit www.oup.com/us/he for the
latest information about pricing and alternate formats.

Published by Oxford University Press.
198 Madison Avenue, New York, New York 10016
http://www.oup.com

Oxford is a registered trademark of Oxford University Press

ISBN 978-0-19-997347-7

9 8 7 6 5

Printed in Canada
on acid-free paper

Contents

Outline Maps

Introduction

THERE ARE MANY WAYS TO TELL A STORY. Textbooks offer narratives, crafted by a modern historian or team of historians. Collections of primary sources present a mosaic of stories, often interspersed with pictures of artwork and other physical objects, drawn from the past. This sort of mosaic allows readers to take a more active role in constructing an overarching story—they recreate something of the process professional historians use to construct their narratives. Narratives and sourcebooks are often excellent at conveying political, social, and cultural developments in particular societies, partly because almost all sources, written or visual (or even archaeological), come from single societies, with travel narratives forming a rare and valuable exception.

This book takes a different approach to telling a story about Western civilization: it presents the West through a series of maps. Maps are not necessarily a better or worse medium for telling a global story. They are simply a different way, a way with its own advantages and disadvantages. Maps usually convey much less detail about the political and cultural details of particular societies than narratives and primary sources can. In addition, maps that adopt a "single-society" approach—the traditional sort of map of a politically defined country's political boundaries and centers of power—sometimes don't add much. They not only reinforce the sort of "nationalist" perspective narratives can lead to but can give a false sense of the independence, coherence, and isolation of such entities.

This book takes advantage of the strengths of maps to tell a different sort of story. Maps can reveal connections by tracing the network connections—of trade, migration, and cultural exchange—and geographic contexts of individual societies. This is valuable because the tension between individual societies, often defined politically, and broader networks, defined economically, socially, and culturally, is arguably one of the central dynamics of world historical development. Maps can also act as snapshots of social history, conveying in dramatic visual terms the aggregate social developments related to demographic and economic growth or change. Like the activities of networks, such deep social trends often do not show up clearly in political narratives or the literary sources generated by social elites. Maps can thus uncover neglected layers of social history. Finally, maps are perhaps the best medium for conveying the trans-regional and even global nature of many such deep processes, from the early emergence of networks of trade through the effect of industrialization on world-wide communications to the impact of global warming on the entire planet.

So, welcome to a story of Western civilization through maps—not a replacement for other stories, but a complementary look, another perspective on a story too vast and rich to be told in just one way.

Mapping *The* Cultures of the West

✳ ✳ ✳

1. The Human Revolution
1 Million Years Ago to 9000 BCE

✳ ✳ ✳

Beginning around 1.8 million years ago hominids spread outside their original home in Africa as far afield as East Asia. Modern humans—*Homo sapiens*—also emerged in Africa and colonized West Africa by 100,000 BCE. The last of the inhabited continents to be colonized by hominids was South America, probably between 14,000 and 11,000 years ago.

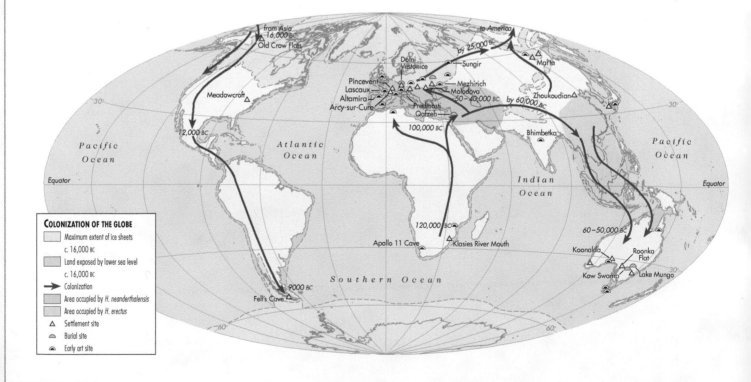

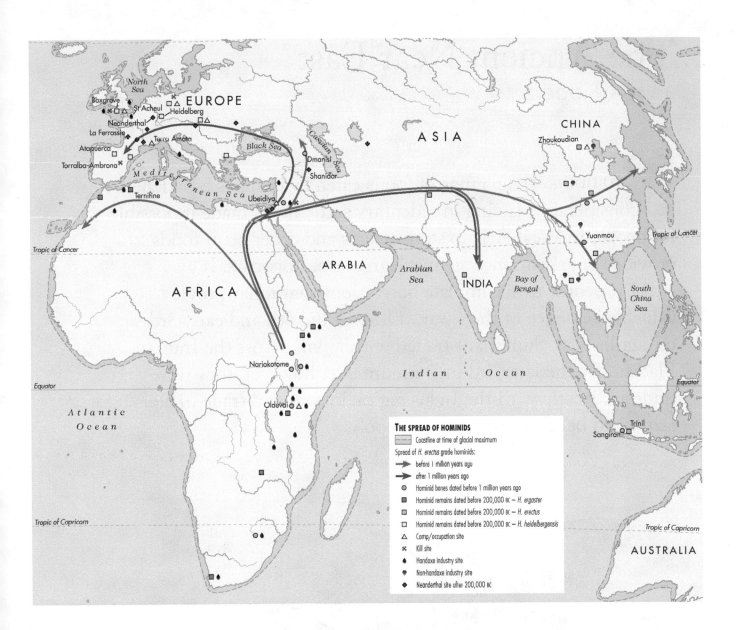

North Sea

Boxgrove
St Acheul   EUROPE
Neanderthal   Heidelberg
La Ferrassie
Atapuerca   Terra Amata
Torralba-Ambrona   *Mediterranean Sea*

CHINA
Zhoukoudian

ASIA

Black Sea
Dmanisi   *Caspian Sea*
Shanidar

Ternifine   Ubeidiya

ARABIA   *Arabian Sea*   INDIA   *Bay of Bengal*

Yuanmou   Tropic of Cancer

Tropic of Cancer

AFRICA

Nariokotome

Indian   Ocean   *South China Sea*

Equator   Equator

Olduvai

Atlantic Ocean

THE SPREAD OF HOMINIDS

Trinil

Sangiran

Tropic of Capricorn

AUSTRALIA

Tropic of Capricorn

THE SPREAD OF HOMINIDS

⬚⬚⬚ Coastline at time of glacial maximum

Spread of *H. erectus* grade hominids:

➤ before 1 million years ago

➤ after 1 million years ago

● Hominid bones dated before 1 million years ago

■ Hominid remains dated before 200,000 BC – *H. ergaster*

■ Hominid remains dated before 200,000 BC – *H. erectus*

□ Hominid remains dated before 200,000 BC – *H. heidelbergensis*

△ Camp/occupation site

✳ Kill site

🝔 Handaxe industry site

🝕 Non-handaxe industry site

◆ Neanderthal site after 200,000 BC

3

2. The Ancient Near East

4000–18,000 BCE

* * *

By 10,000 BCE the range of foods eaten by humans broadened considerably. Living in sedentary settlements made it possible for people in West Asia to store cereals and other plant foods to provide some insurance against lean seasons or years. It also enabled people to accumulate possessions that today provide valuable evidence of their way of life. In the 4th and early 3rd millennia BCE, Sumerians traded with towns across the Iranian Plateau. By the later 3rd millennium BCE, however, they were trading directly with the Indus region by sea, and trade in lapis lazuli had become an Indus monopoly.

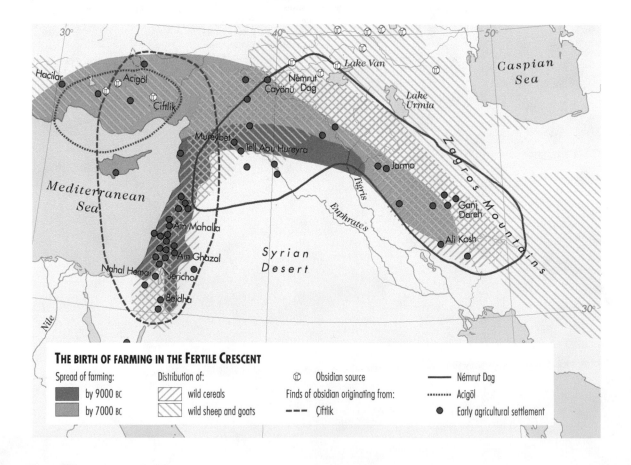

THE BIRTH OF FARMING IN THE FERTILE CRESCENT

Spread of farming:
- by 9000 BC
- by 7000 BC

Distribution of:
- wild cereals
- wild sheep and goats

- Obsidian source
- Finds of obsidian originating from:
  - --- Çiftlik

- —— Némrut Dag
- ········ Acigöl
- ● Early agricultural settlement

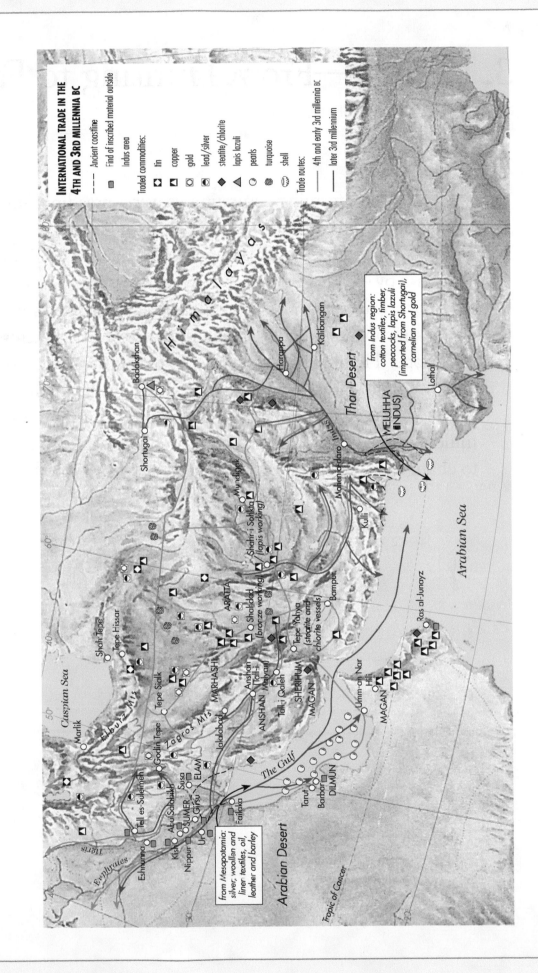

INTERNATIONAL TRADE IN THE 4TH AND 3RD MILLENNIA BC

Ancient coastline

◼ Find of inscribed material outside
Indus area

Traded commodities:
◻ tin
◻ copper
◻ gold
◆ lead/silver
◆ steatite/chlorite
▲ lapis lazuli
○ pearls
◉ turquoise
⬭ shell

Trade routes:
— 4th and early 3rd millennia BC
— later 3rd millennium

from Indus region: cotton textiles, timber, peacocks, lapis lazuli (imported from Shortugai), carnelian and gold

from Mesopotamia: silver, woollen and linen textiles, oil, leather and barley

Himalayas

Thar Desert

MELUHHA (INDUS)

Badakshan

Shortugai

Harappa

Kalibangan

Lothal

Mundigak

Mohenjo-daro (Indus)

Shahr-i Sokhta (lapis working)

Kulli

ARATTA

Shahdad (bronze working)

Tepe Yahya (steatite and chlorite vessels)

Bampur

Ras al-Junayz

Shah Tepe

Tepe Hissar

Tepe Sialk

MARHASHI

Shahr-i

ANSHAN (Malyan)

Anshan (Tall-i Malyan)

Tall-i Qaleh

SHERIHUM

MAGAN

Umm-an Nar

Hili

MAGAN

Marlik

Caspian Sea

Elburz Mts

Zagros Mts

Godin Tepe

Tell es-Suleimeh

Jalalabad

ELAM

Susa

Arabian Sea

The Gulf

Tanut

Barbar

DILMUN

Eshnunna

Abu Salabikh

SUMER

Kish

Nippur

Girsu

Ur

Failaka

Tigris

Euphrates

Arabian Desert

Tropic of Cancer

5

3. Europe—From Hunting to Farming
8000–800 BCE

* * *

By 7000 BCE farming communities were spreading from Anatolia into southeast Europe, bringing with them wheat, barley, sheep, and goats. Farming also spread into neighboring areas and by 4000 BCE was widespread across the continent, though the greater part of Europe was still sparsely inhabited forest. By 3000 BCE copper and gold metallurgy were practiced across most of Europe. These metals were used to make prestige goods that enhanced the status of high-ranking individuals. Small-scale chiefdoms emerged in many parts of Europe during the 2nd millennium BCE. Around 1130 BCE, however, this situation began to change, culminating in the larger groupings of the Iron Age.

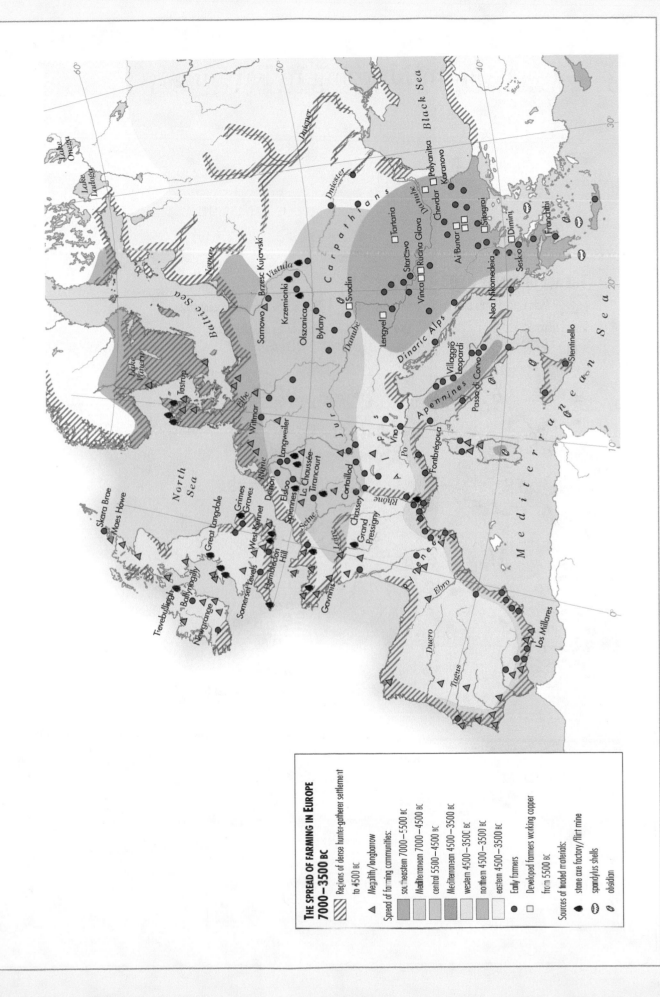

THE SPREAD OF FARMING IN EUROPE
7000–3500 BC

Regions of dense hunter-gatherer settlement
to 4500 BC

▲ Megalith/longbarrow

Spread of farming communities:
southeastern 7000–5500 BC
Mediterranean 7000–4500 BC
central 5500–4500 BC
Mediterranean 4500–3500 BC
western 4500–3500 BC
northern 4500–3500 BC
eastern 4500–3500 BC

● Early farmers

□ Developed farmers working copper
from 5500 BC

Sources of traded materials:
● stone axe factory/flint mine
◈ spondylus shells
⊘ obsidian

Labels on map:
Lake Onega
Lake Ladoga
Baltic Sea
Black Sea
North Sea
Mediterranean Sea
Dniester
Dnieper
Niemen
Vistula
Danube
Carpathians
Dinaric Alps
Apennines
Alps
Jura
Rhine
Elbe
Seine
Loire
Rhône
Po
Ebro
Duero
Tagus
Pyrenees

Polyanitsa
Karanovo
Chevdar
Sitagroi
Tartaria
Starčevo
Ručna Glava
Vinca
Ai Bunar
Dimini
Sesklo
Franchthi
Nea Nikomedeia
Lengyel
Svodin
Bylany
Olszanica
Krzemionki
Sarnowo
Brzesc Kujawski
Villaggio Leopardi
Passo di Corvo
Stentinello
Fontbrégoua
Chassey
Grand Pressigny
Cortaillod
La Chaussée-Tirancourt
Spiennes
Elsloo
Deiron
Langweiler
Wittmar
Tustrop
Grimes Graves
Great Langdale
West Kennet
Hambledon Hill
Somerset levels
Skara Brae
Maes Howe
Trevebulliagh
Ballynagilly
Newgrange
Gavrinis
Los Millares

7

3. Europe: From Hunting to Farming

8000–800 BCE

* * *

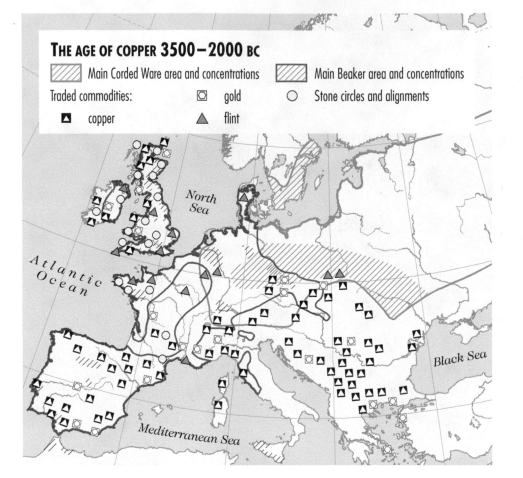

THE AGE OF COPPER 3500–2000 BC

Main Corded Ware area and concentrations

Main Beaker area and concentrations

Traded commodities:

gold

Stone circles and alignments

copper

flint

North Sea

Atlantic Ocean

Black Sea

Mediterranean Sea

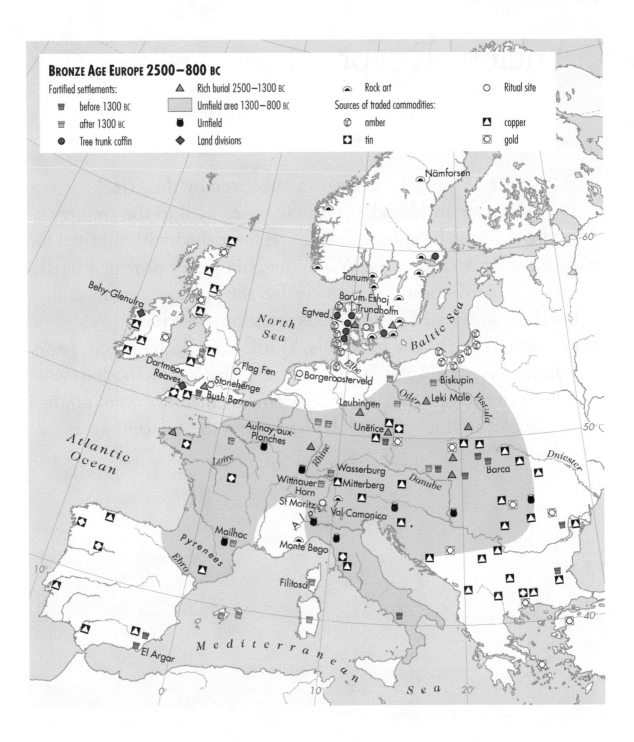

BRONZE AGE EUROPE 2500–800 BC

Fortified settlements:

🏰 before 1300 BC

🏰 after 1300 BC

⬤ Tree trunk coffin

🔺 Rich burial 2500–1300 BC

▨ Urnfield area 1300–800 BC

⬛ Urnfield

◆ Land divisions

🌙 Rock art

Sources of traded commodities:

⊕ amber

⬧ tin

○ Ritual site

🔺 copper

◨ gold

Nämforsen

Tanum

Borum Eshoj
Trundholm

Egtved

Behy-Glenulra

*North
Sea*

Baltic Sea

Elbe

Bargeroosterveld

Biskupin

Flag Fen

Dartmoor
Reaves

Stonehenge

Bush Barrow

Leubingen

Oder

Lęki Małe

Vistula

Aulnay-aux-
Planches

Unĕtice

*Atlantic
Ocean*

Loire

Rhine

Wasserburg

Danube

Barca

Dniester

Wittnauer
Horn

Mitterberg

St Moritz

Val Camonica

Mailhac

Pyrenees

Monte Bego

Ebro

Filitosa

El Argar

M e d i t e r r a n e a n   S e a

60

50°

10°

40

0

10

20

4. Ancient Egypt

2686–1069 BCE

* * *

"Gift of the Nile" was the name given by the Greek historian Herodotus (ca. 485–425 BCE) to the country where Ancient Egyptian civilization flourished without rival for over two thousand years. While the Nile Valley provided fertile soils, the surrounding deserts yielded the precious metals and building stone used in ambitious artistic and architectural endeavors such as the pyramids. While the Old Kingdom period is known as the "Age of the Pyramids," the New Kingdom was the era of the vast temples and lavishly painted tombs of pharaohs and nobles in the Valley of the Kings and the adjacent areas around Thebes.

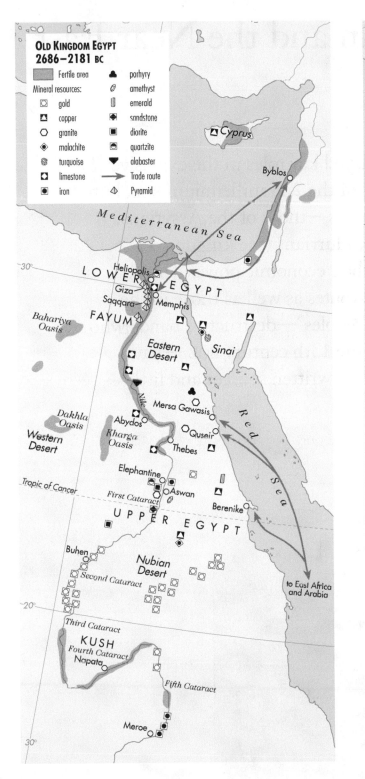

OLD KINGDOM EGYPT
2686–2181 BC

▨	Fertile area	
Mineral resources:		▲ porhyry
▨ gold		⦾ amethyst
⬛ copper		▯ emerald
⬠ granite		◈ sandstone
◈ malachite		▣ diorite
✿ turquoise		⬓ quartzite
⬕ limestone		▼ alabaster
◉ iron		→ Trade route
		◇ Pyramid

Mediterranean Sea

Cyprus

Byblos

LOWER EGYPT
Heliopolis
Giza
Saqqara — Memphis
FAYUM
Bahariya Oasis

Eastern Desert
Sinai

Dakhla Oasis
Western Desert
Abydos
Kharga Oasis
Thebes
Mersa Gawasis
Quseir

Red Sea

Elephantine
Aswan
First Cataract
Tropic of Cancer
Berenike

UPPER EGYPT

Nubian Desert
Buhen
Second Cataract

to East Africa and Arabia

Third Cataract
KUSH
Fourth Cataract
Napata
Fifth Cataract

Meroe

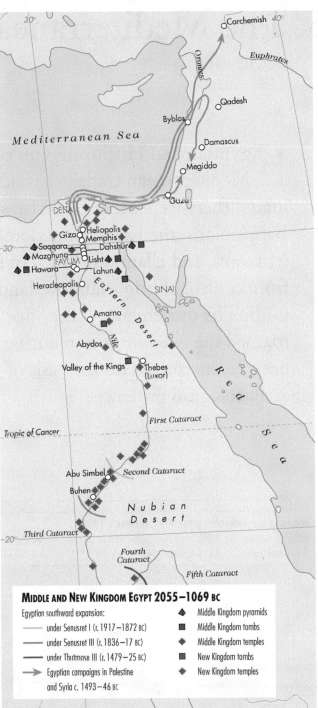

MIDDLE AND NEW KINGDOM EGYPT 2055–1069 BC

Egyptian southward expansion:
- under Senusret I (r. 1917–1872 BC)
- under Senusret III (r. 1836–17 BC)
- under Thutmose III (r. 1479–25 BC)
- → Egyptian campaigns in Palestine and Syria c. 1493–46 BC

- ◆ Middle Kingdom pyramids
- ■ Middle Kingdom tombs
- ✦ Middle Kingdom temples
- ▪ New Kingdom tombs
- ✚ New Kingdom temples

Carchemish
Euphrates
Orontes
Qadesh
Byblos
Damascus
Megiddo
Guzu

Mediterranean Sea

DELTA
Giza — Heliopolis
Saqqara — Memphis
Mazghuna — Dahshur
FAYUM — Lisht
Hawara — Lahun
Heracleopolis

SINAI

Eastern Desert

Amarna
Abydos

Valley of the Kings
Thebes (Luxor)

First Cataract
Tropic of Cancer

Red Sea

Abu Simbel — Second Cataract
Buhen

Nubian Desert

Third Cataract

Fourth Cataract

Fifth Cataract

5. The Mediterranean and the Near East
2000–1000 BCE

✳ ✳ ✳

Egyptian and Hittite empires played key roles in the extensive Mediterranean trade networks of the 2nd millennium BCE, but inland there were other powerful states—those of the Assyrians, Babylonians (the Kassite kingdom), Hurrians (the kingdom of Mitanni), and Elamites. Much of their economic power derived from control of important overland routes as well as those in the Gulf. The movements of the "Sea Peoples"—destructive bands who roamed the Mediterranean during the 13th century BCE —have been reconstructed on the basis of few written sources and little archaeological evidence.

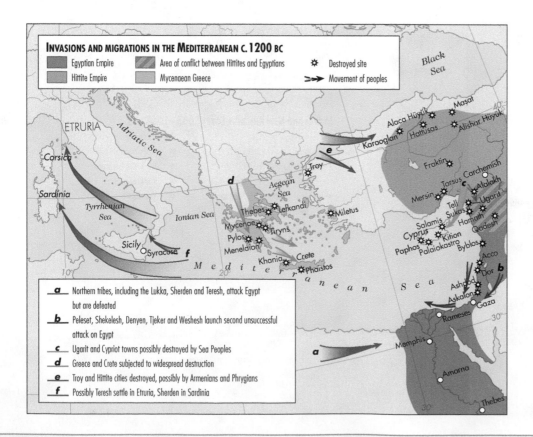

INVASIONS AND MIGRATIONS IN THE MEDITERRANEAN C. 1200 BC

- Egyptian Empire
- Hittite Empire
- Area of conflict between Hittites and Egyptians
- Mycenaean Greece
- ✳ Destroyed site
- ➤➤ Movement of peoples

a Northern tribes, including the Lukka, Sherden and Teresh, attack Egypt but are defeated
b Peleset, Shekelesh, Denyen, Tjeker and Weshesh launch second unsuccessful attack on Egypt
c Ugarit and Cypriot towns possibly destroyed by Sea Peoples
d Greece and Crete subjected to widespread destruction
e Troy and Hittite cities destroyed, possibly by Armenians and Phrygians
f Possibly Teresh settle in Etruria, Sherden in Sardinia

6. Empires and Traders

1200–600 BCE

✳ ✳ ✳

The Phoenicians emerged as a major sea trading nation in the 1st millennium BCE. In the early 8th century BCE waning Assyrian power allowed neighboring kingdoms, such as the Urartians and the Chaldeans, to prosper. Assyrian power grew once again in the late 8th century BCE, and after gaining control of Babylonia and the Levant it made a partially successful attack on Egypt in 671 BCE. Within just fifty years, however, Assyria itself was attacked and subdued by the Babylonians.

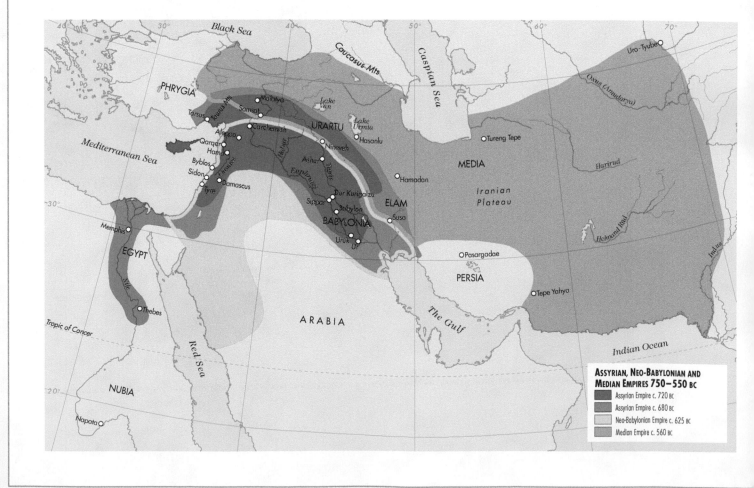

ASSYRIAN, NEO-BABYLONIAN AND MEDIAN EMPIRES 750–550 BC

- Assyrian Empire c. 720 BC
- Assyrian Empire c. 680 BC
- Neo-Babylonian Empire c. 625 BC
- Median Empire c. 560 BC

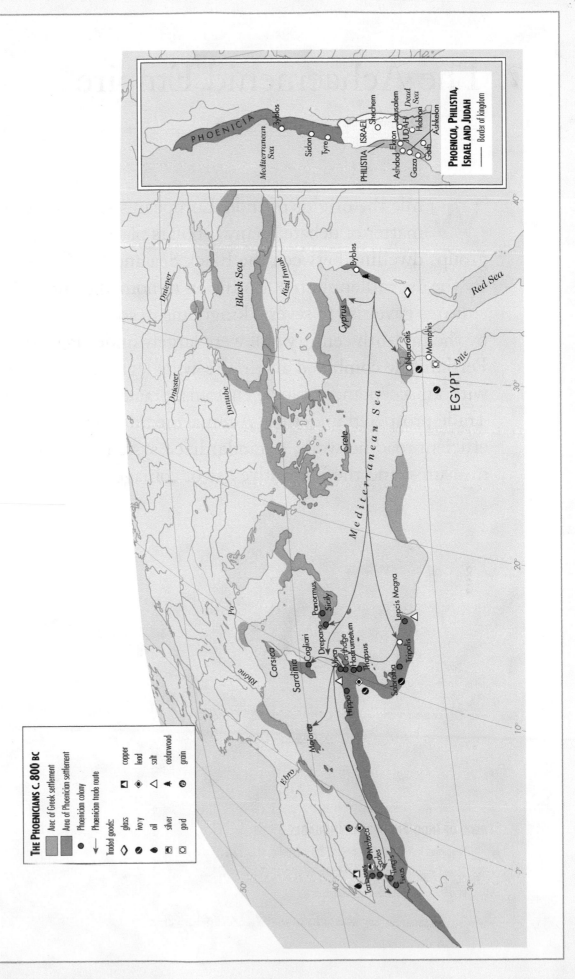

THE PHOENICIANS C. 800 BC

Area of Greek settlement
Area of Phoenician settlement
● Phoenician colony
↓ Phoenician trade route

Traded goods:

◇ glass   ◪ copper
◕ ivory   ◈ lead
◑ oil   △ salt
◪ silver   ♠ cedarwood
▣ gold   ✸ grain

PHOENICIA, PHILISTIA, ISRAEL AND JUDAH
—— Border of kingdom

PHOENICIA
Mediterranean Sea
Byblos
Sidon
Tyre
Shechem
Jerusalem
Dead Sea
ISRAEL
Ekron
JUDAH
PHILISTIA
Ashdod
Hebron
Gath
Gaza
Ashkelon

Red Sea
Black Sea
Dnieper
Dniester
Danube
Kizil Irmak
Byblos
Cyprus
Naucratis
Memphis
Nile
EGYPT
Crete
Mediterranean Sea
Po
Rhône
Corsica
Sardinia
Majorca
Ebro
Cagliari
Drepana
Panormus
Sicily
Utica
Carthage
Hadrumetum
Thapsus
Hippo
Sabratha
Tripolis
Lepcis Magna
Malaca
Gades
Tingis
Lixus
Tartessus

15

7. The Achaemenid Empire

550–525 BCE

✳ ✳ ✳

While the origins of Indo-European speakers are still a matter of debate, many scholars place them among the groups dwelling between the Black Sea and the Caspian Sea. By the 1st millennium BCE a fusion of nomadic and sedentary cultures gave rise to several kingdoms in southeast Asia, which by the mid-6th century BCE were largely under Persian rule. Persian rule combined an empire-wide legal administrative system with an acceptance of local customs, practices, and religions. Trade prospered under the Achmaemenids, facilitated by an efficient road network, a standardized system of weights and measures, and the innovative use of coinage.

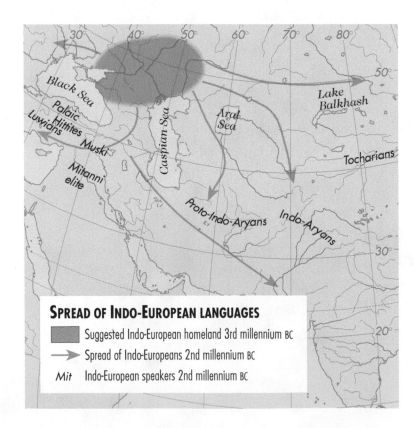

SPREAD OF INDO-EUROPEAN LANGUAGES

▨ Suggested Indo-European homeland 3rd millennium BC

→ Spread of Indo-Europeans 2nd millennium BC

Mit Indo-European speakers 2nd millennium BC

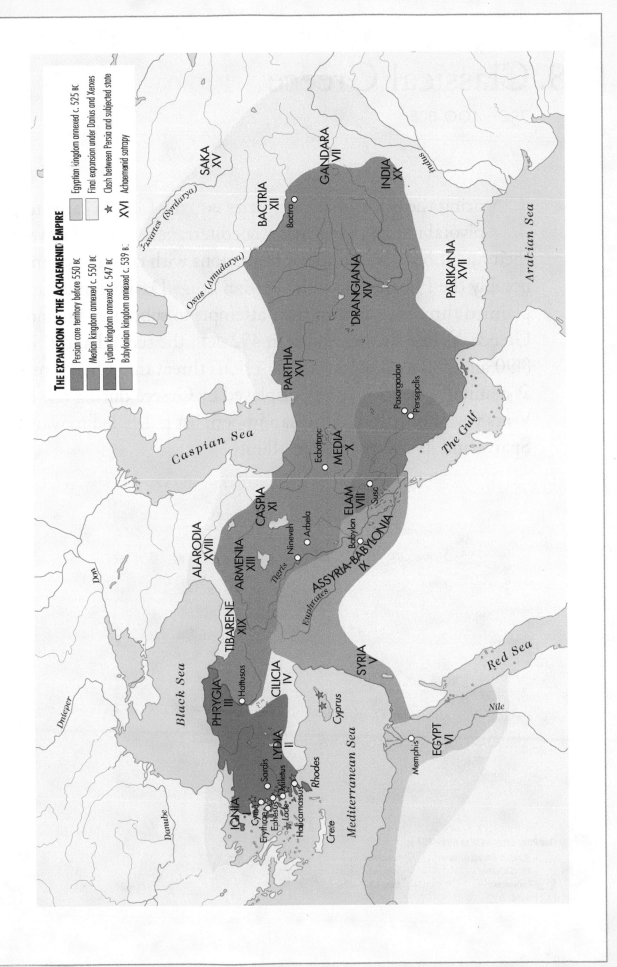

THE EXPANSION OF THE ACHAEMENID EMPIRE

Persian core territory before 550 BC
Median kingdom annexed c. 550 BC
Lydian kingdom annexed c. 547 BC
Babylonian kingdom annexed c. 539 BC
Egyptian kingdom annexed c. 525 BC
Final expansion under Darius and Xerxes
★ Clash between Persia and subjected state
XVI Achaemenid satrapy

Iaxartes (Syrdarya)

SAKA
XV

GANDARA
VII

BACTRIA
XII
Bactra

INDIA
XX

Indus

Oxus (Amudarya)

PARIKANIA
XVII

DRANGIANA
XIV

Aralian Sea

PARTHIA
XVI

Pasargadae
Persepolis

Caspian Sea

Ecbatana
MEDIA
X

The Gulf

CASPIA
XI

ELAM
VIII
Susa

ALARODIA
XVIII

Arbela

Babylon
BABYLONIA

ARMENIA
XIII

Nineveh

ASSYRIA-BABYLONIA
IX

Don

Tigris

TIBARENE
XIX

Euphrates

Black Sea

SYRIA
V

Red Sea

PHRYGIA
III
Hattusas

CILICIA
IV

Nile

Dnieper

LYDIA
II

Cyprus

EGYPT
VI
Memphis

Sardis
Cyme
Erythrae
Ephesus
Miletus
Lade
Halicarnassus

IONIA

Rhodes

Crete

Mediterranean Sea

Danube

17

8. Classical Greece

750–400 BCE

✳ ✳ ✳

During the 8th and 7th centuries BCE the Greeks came to play a pivotal role in the growing Mediterranean trade. However, their ambitions also led to confrontations with rival merchant forces, notably the Phoenicians. The Persian kings Darius I and Xerxes planned three invasions in their attempts to subdue mainland Greece. While the first failed in 492 BCE, the second and third (490 and 480 BCE) posed such a serious threat that Greece responded as a united force. The unity displayed by Greece during the Persian Wars was short-lived. Athenian imperialist policy led to war with Sparta and its Peloponnesian allies.

THE PELOPONNESIAN WAR 431–404 BC

Athens and Delian League members	Persian Empire
Area allied to Athens	✕ Athenian victory with date
Sparta and allies	✕ Spartan victory with date
Neutral area	

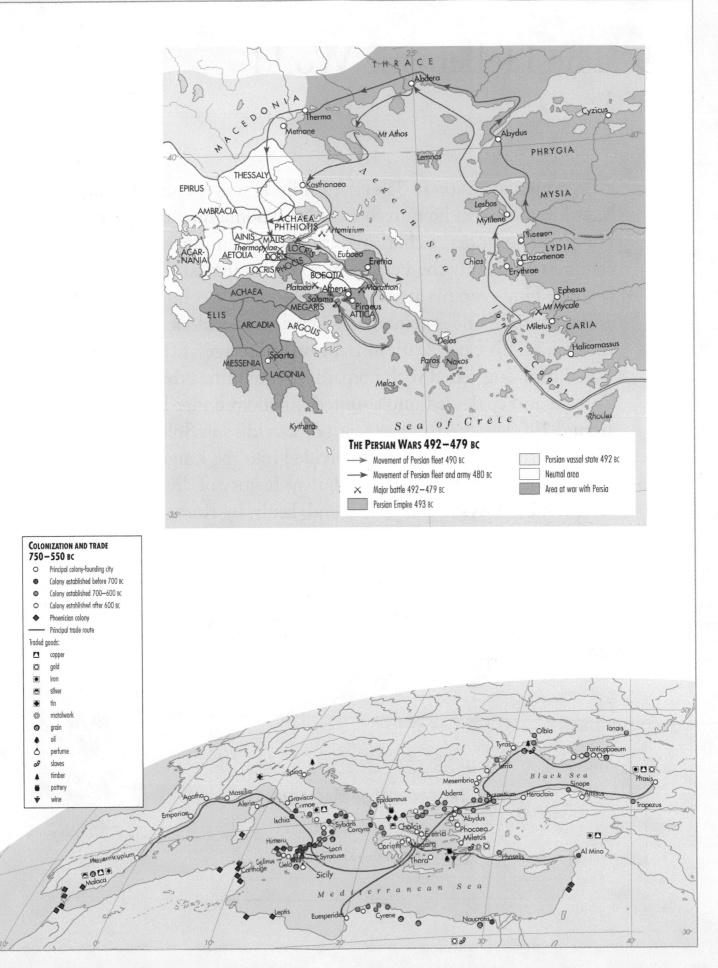

THE PERSIAN WARS 492–479 BC

→ Movement of Persian fleet 490 BC
→ Movement of Persian fleet and army 480 BC
✕ Major battle 492–479 BC

Persian Empire 493 BC
Persian vassal state 492 BC
Neutral area
Area at war with Persia

COLONIZATION AND TRADE 750–550 BC

○ Principal colony-founding city
● Colony established before 700 BC
◐ Colony established 700–600 BC
○ Colony established after 600 BC
◆ Phoenician colony
— Principal trade route

Traded goods:
△ copper
◉ gold
◉ iron
◉ silver
◈ tin
⊛ metalwork
◉ grain
◆ oil
◊ perfume
◔ slaves
▲ timber
▮ pottery
▽ wine

9. The Hellenistic World

334–275 BCE

✳ ✳ ✳

On his succession in 359 BCE, Philip II was master of a tiny kingdom, yet he transformed Macedonia into a major power. His son, Alexander, a charismatic leader and military genius, conquered not only the Persian Empire but also lands well beyond. However, his attempts to weld his vast conquests into a unified empire under combined Macedonian and local rulers ended with his early death in Babylon at the age of thirty-two.

Judaism originated with nomadic communities that settled in Canaan and coalesced into a united kingdom under King David around 1000 BCE. After the death of David's son Solomon in 926 BCE, the Jewish lands were divided into the kingdoms of Israel and Judah, which then had a turbulent history of division and conquest by Assyria, Babylonia, and, lastly, by Rome.

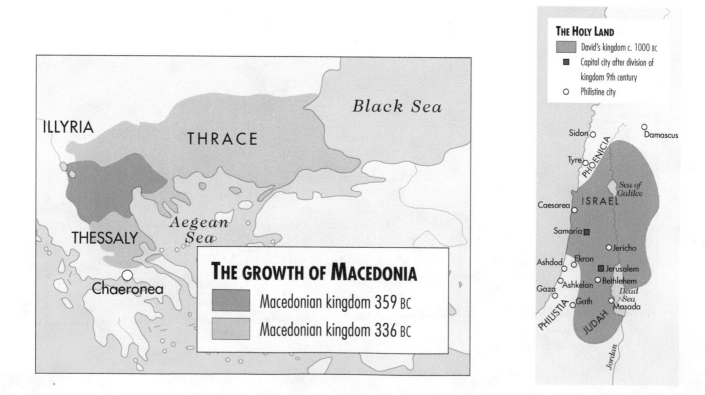

THE HOLY LAND
David's kingdom c. 1000 BC
Capital city after division of kingdom 9th century
Philistine city

THE GROWTH OF MACEDONIA
Macedonian kingdom 359 BC
Macedonian kingdom 336 BC

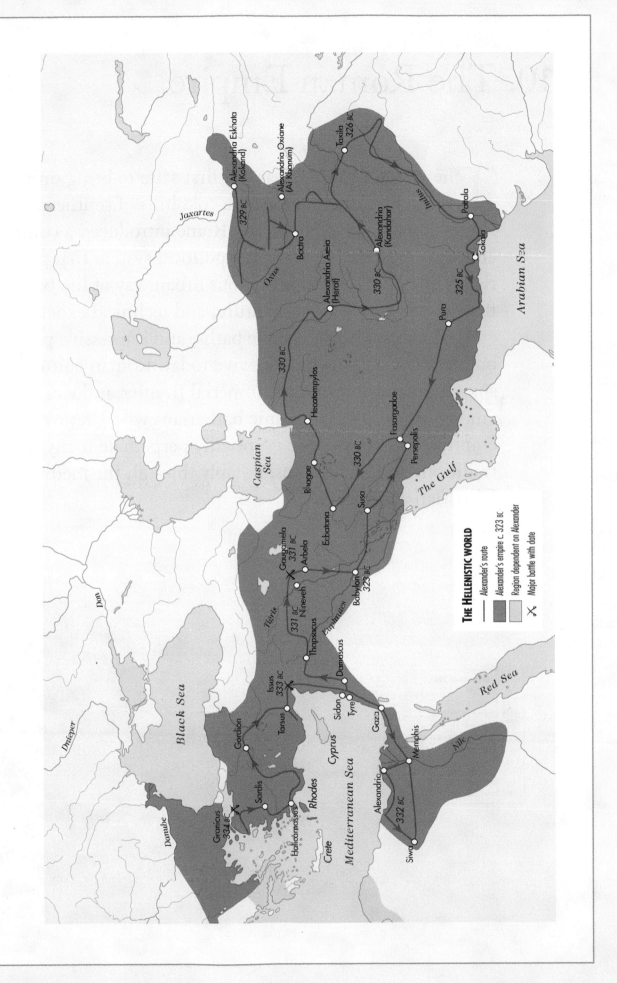

THE HELLENISTIC WORLD

Alexander's route

Alexander's empire c. 323 BC

Region dependent on Alexander

✗ Major battle with date

Jaxartes

Alexandria Eskhata (Kokand)

Alexandria Oxiane (Ai Khanum)

329 BC

Taxila 326 BC

Pattala

Bactra

Oxus

Indus

Kokala

Alexandria (Kandahar)

Alexandria Areia (Herat)

330 BC

325 BC

Arabian Sea

330 BC

Pura

Hecatompylos

Caspian Sea

Pasargadae

330 BC

Persepolis

Ecbatana

Susa

The Gulf

Gaugamela 331 BC

Arbela

Nineveh

331 BC

Tigris

Babylon 323 BC

Euphrates

Thapsacus

Don

Damascus

Issus 333 BC

Sidon

Tyre

Red Sea

Tarsus

Gaza

Dnieper

Black Sea

Gordion

Memphis

Nile

Sardis

Cyprus

Alexandria

Granicus 334 BC

Rhodes

332 BC

Halicarnassus

Crete

Mediterranean Sea

Danube

Siwa

10. The Roman Empire

* * *

The Roman Empire was the first state to bring unity to much of Europe. From the cold hills of southern Scotland to the deserts of North Africa, Rome introduced a common culture, language, and script; a political system that gave equal rights to all citizens; a prosperous urban way of life backed by flourishing trade and agriculture; and technical expertise that created roads, bridges, public baths, and impressive public buildings, some of which survive today. Roman culture also spread to lands beyond the imperial frontier, influencing, among others, the Germanic barbarians who later overran the empire—but who would eventually perpetuate many of its traditions and institutions, notably through the medium of the Christian church.

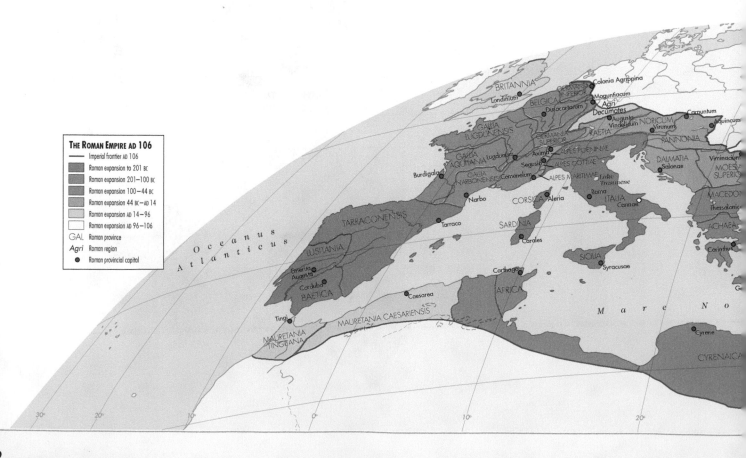

THE ROMAN EMPIRE AD 106
- Imperial frontier AD 106
- Roman expansion to 201 BC
- Roman expansion 201–100 BC
- Roman expansion 100–44 BC
- Roman expansion 44 BC–AD 14
- Roman expansion AD 14–96
- Roman expansion AD 96–106

GAL Roman province
Agri Roman region
● Roman provincial capital

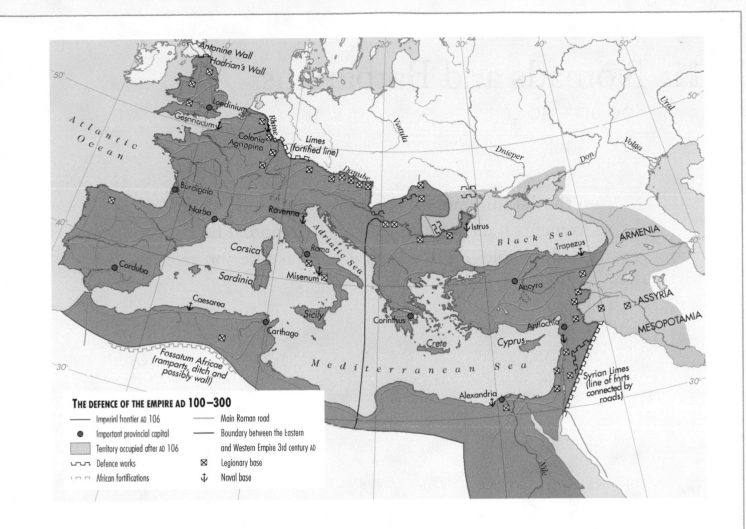

THE DEFENCE OF THE EMPIRE AD 100–300

- —— Imperial frontier AD 106
- ● Important provincial capital
- Territory occupied after AD 106
- Defence works
- African fortifications
- —— Main Roman road
- —— Boundary between the Eastern and Western Empire 3rd century AD
- ⊠ Legionary base
- ⚓ Naval base

Labels on map:
Antonine Wall, Hadrian's Wall, Londinium, Gesoriacum, Colonia Agrippina, Limes (fortified line), Rhine, Danube, Vistula, Dnieper, Don, Volga, Ural, Atlantic Ocean, Burdigala, Narbo, Ravenna, Corsica, Sardinia, Roma, Adriatic Sea, Misenum, Corduba, Caesarea, Carthago, Sicily, Crete, Corinthus, Cyprus, Mediterranean Sea, Black Sea, Trapezus, ARMENIA, Ancyra, ASSYRIA, MESOPOTAMIA, Antiochia, Syrian Limes (line of forts connected by roads), Alexandria, Nile, Istrus, Fossatum Africae (ramparts, ditch and possibly wall)

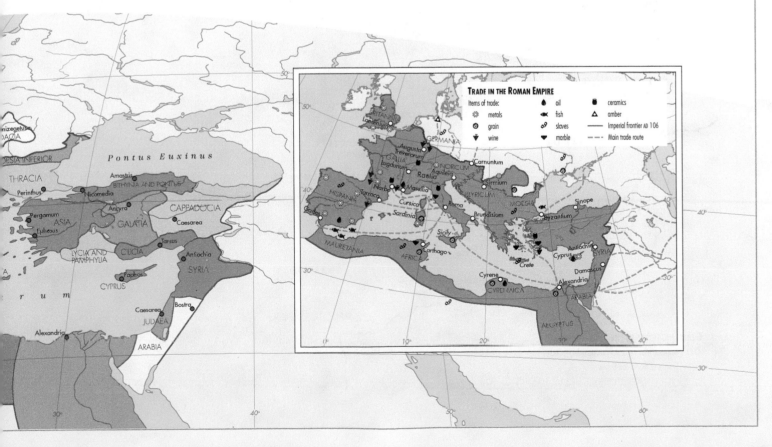

TRADE IN THE ROMAN EMPIRE

Items of trade:
- ● oil
- metals
- grain
- wine
- fish
- slaves
- marble
- ceramics
- △ amber
- —— Imperial frontier AD 106
- – – – Main trade route

Labels on maps:
Pontus Euxinus, THRACIA, Perinthus, Amastris, Nicomedia, Ancyra, CAPPADOCIA, Pergamum, ASIA, GALATIA, Ephesus, LYCIA AND PAMPHYLIA, CILICIA, Tarsus, CYPRUS, Paphos, Antiochia, SYRIA, Caesarea, Bostra, JUDAEA, ARABIA, Alexandria

BRITANNIA, Londinium, GERMANIA, Augusta Treverorum, Lugdunum, GALLIA, Raetia, NORICUM, Aquileia, Carnuntum, Narbo, Massilia, Sirmium, ILLYRICUM, HISPANIA, Tarraco, Corsica, Roma, MOESIA, Sinope, Gades, Sardinia, Brundisium, Byzantium, MAURETANIA, Sicily, Crete, Antiochia, Cyprus, SYRIA, Damascus, AFRICA, Carthago, Cyrene, CYRENAICA, Alexandria, ARABIA, AEGYPTUS

11. Nomads and Barbarians
800 BCE–350 CE

✳ ✳ ✳

From the 1st millennium BCE substantial population movements took place in the steppe region. The Romans regarded all peoples outside their empire as inferior, referring to them as "barbarians."

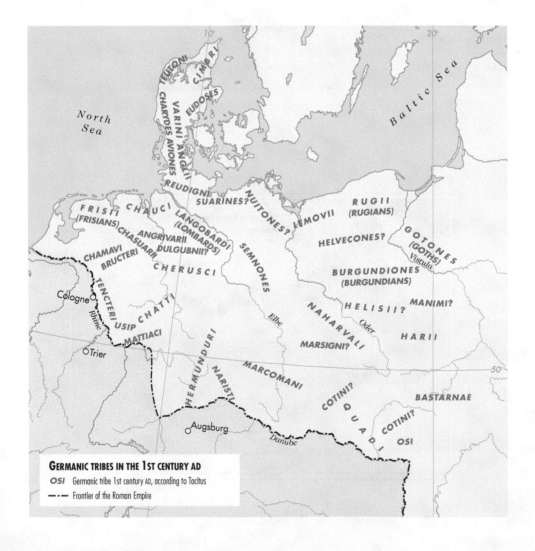

GERMANIC TRIBES IN THE 1ST CENTURY AD

OSI   Germanic tribe 1st century AD, according to Tacitus

–·–· Frontier of the Roman Empire

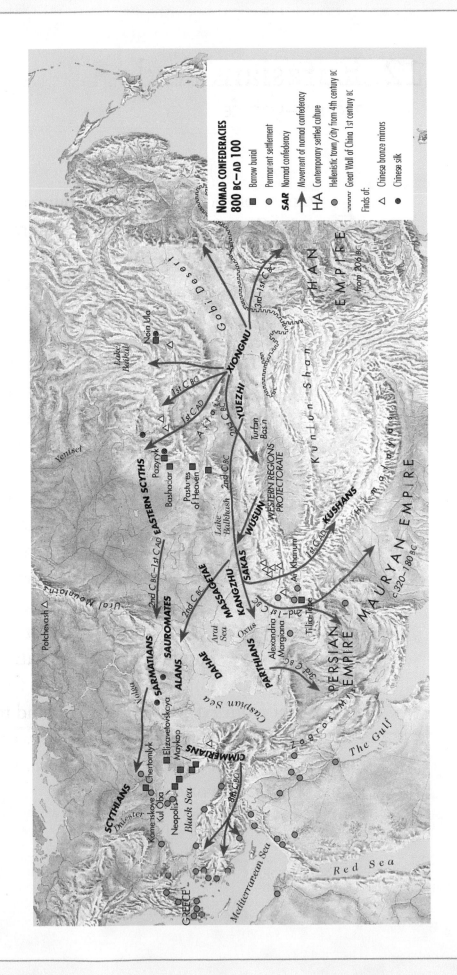

NOMAD CONFEDERACIES
800 BC–AD 100

■ Barrow burial
● Permanent settlement
SAR Nomad confederacy
↑ Movement of nomad confederacy
HA Contemporary settled culture
● Hellenistic town/city from 4th century BC
⌐⌐⌐ Great Wall of China 1st century BC

Finds of:
△ Chinese bronze mirrors
● Chinese silk

Gobi Desert

Lake Baikal

Noin Ula

Yenisei

3rd–1st C BC

HAN EMPIRE
from 206 BC

1st C BC

1st C AD

Pazyryk

Bashadar

Pastures of Heaven

XIONGNU

YUEZHI

Altai

2nd C BC

Turfan Basin

EASTERN SCYTHS

2nd C BC–1st C AD

Lake Balkhash

WUSUN

WESTERN REGIONS PROTECTORATE

Kunlun Shan

Himalayas

SAKAS

KANGZHU

KUSHANS

1st C AD

Ai Khanum

Ural Mountains

Potchevash △

SARMATIANS

SAUROMATES

ALANS

DAHAE

MASSAGETAE

2nd C BC

Volga

Aral Sea

Oxus

2nd–1st C BC

Tillia Tepe

PARTHIANS

Alexandria Margiana

3rd C BC

MAURYAN EMPIRE
c.320–180 BC

PERSIAN EMPIRE

Caspian Sea

Zagros Mts

The Gulf

Chertomlyk

Kamenskoye

Elizavetovskaya

Maykop

Kul Oba

Neapolis

SCYTHIANS

Dniester

CIMMERIANS

8th C BC

Black Sea

Mediterranean Sea

GREECE

Red Sea

25

12. Eurasian Trade

150 BCE–500 CE

* * *

A variety of routes linked the countries of Asia, East Africa, and the Mediterranean. Long-established routes through the Gulf and across the Iranian Plateau flourished during the 1st millennium BCE under the Achaemenids and their Hellenistic successors. From the 2nd century BCE the newly established Chinese trade route across Central Asia linked with these existing routes, while Arabs and Indians operated sea trade across the Indian Ocean, and desert caravans carried incense from southern Arabia via the Nabataean state to Rome. By the 1st century CE hostility between the Parthian and Roman empires had closed the overland route through Persia, and the Romans became directly involved in Indian Ocean trade. During the reign of Augustus trade became Rome's lifeline. To feed its rapidly expanding urban population, it depended on the import of grain—first from Sicily, later from Africa and Egypt—and to suit the tastes of Rome's elite luxury goods were imported from even further afield, including silk from China and ivory from Africa.

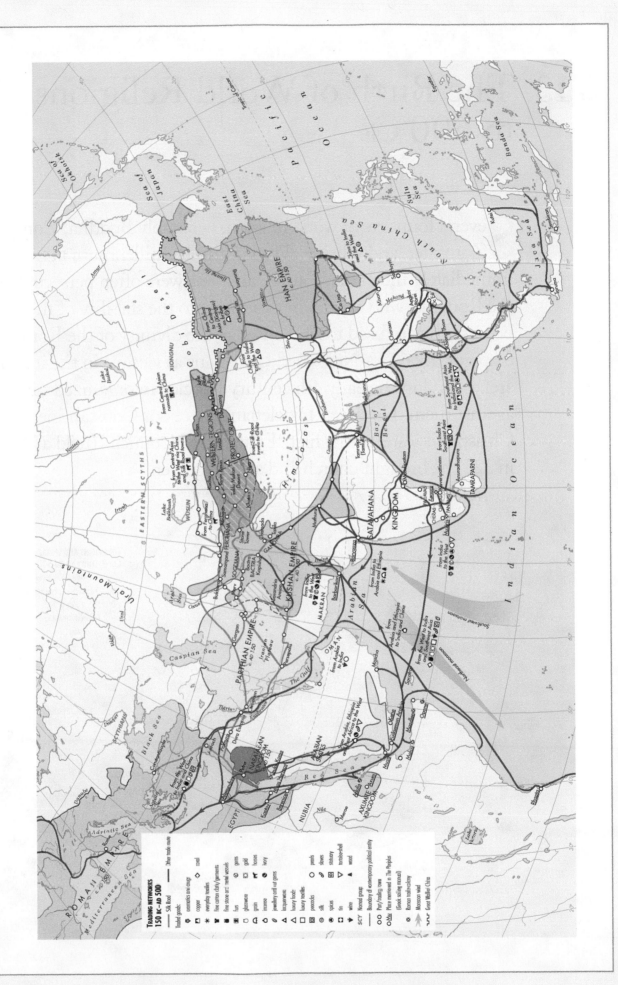

13. The Birth of World Religions to 600 CE

✳ ✳ ✳

Several founders of world religions—notably Buddha, Confucius, Zoroaster, and Christ—lived in the 1st millennium BCE or immediately thereafter. Early Christians were often persecuted by the Romans, who saw them as a threat to the stability of the empire because they refused to acknowledge the divinity of the Roman emperor. By 64 CE Nero used Christians as victims in the imperial arenas, and in the early 4th century Diocletian organized campaigns against them. However, Diocletian's successor Constantine legalized Christianity, and at the first "Ecumenical Council" (held at Nicaea in 325) he brought church and state together. ◆

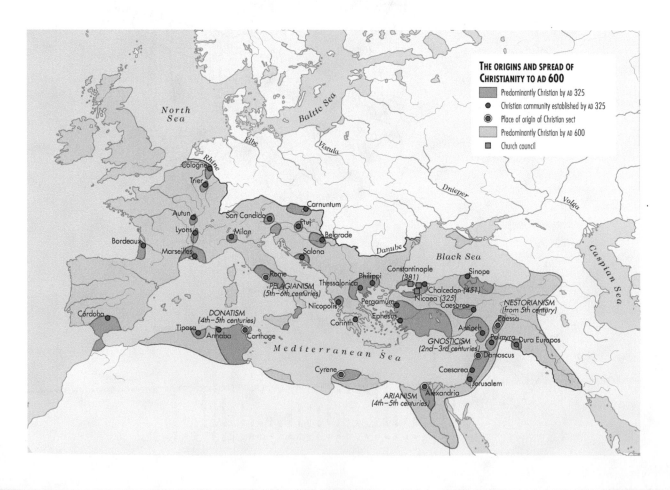

THE ORIGINS AND SPREAD OF CHRISTIANITY TO AD 600

Predominantly Christian by AD 325
● Christian community established by AD 325
◉ Place of origin of Christian sect
Predominantly Christian by AD 600
◼ Church council

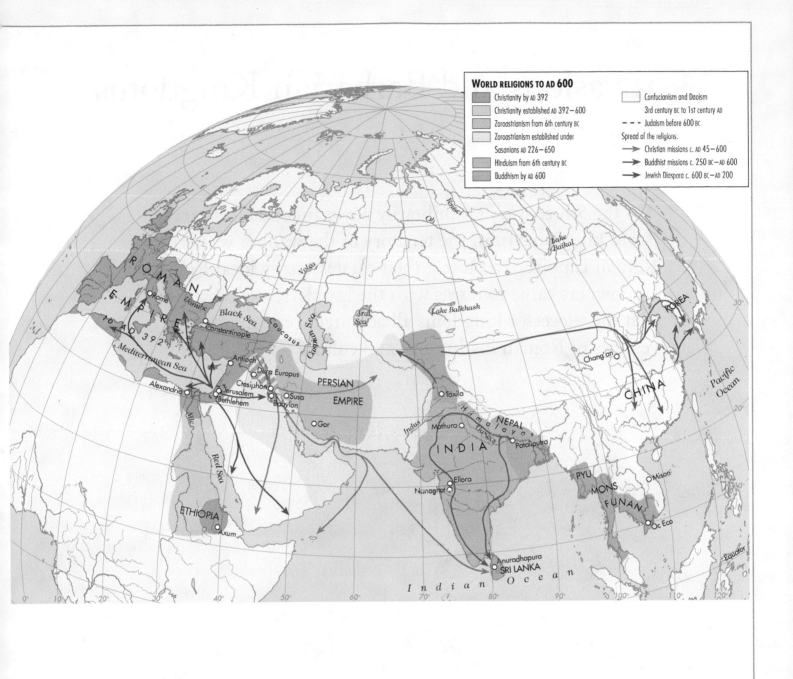

WORLD RELIGIONS TO AD 600

- Christianity by AD 392
- Christianity established AD 392—600
- Zoroastrianism from 6th century BC
- Zoroastrianism established under Sasanians AD 226—650
- Hinduism from 6th century BC
- Buddhism by AD 600
- Confucianism and Daoism 3rd century BC to 1st century AD
- - - Judaism before 600 BC

Spread of the religions:
- → Christian missions c. AD 45—600
- → Buddhist missions c. 250 BC—AD 600
- → Jewish Diaspora c. 600 BC—AD 200

ROMAN EMPIRE to AD 392

Rome

Danube

Black Sea

Constantinople

Caucasus

Antioch

Dura Europus

Mediterranean Sea

Alexandria

Ctesiphon

Jerusalem

Bethlehem

Susa

Babylon

PERSIAN EMPIRE

Gor

Nile

Red Sea

ETHIOPIA

Axum

Volga

Aral Sea

Caspian Sea

Lake Balkhash

Yenisei

Ob

Lake Baikal

Chang'an

CHINA

KOREA

Pacific Ocean

Taxila

Himalaya

NEPAL

Mathura

Ganges

Indus

INDIA

Pataliputra

Ellora

Nanaghat

PYU

MONS

FUNAN

Mison

Oc Eco

Anuradhapura

SRI LANKA

Indian Ocean

Equator

14. Invasions and Barbarian Kingdoms

375–500 CE

✳ ✳ ✳

In the 5th century CE militarily powerful outsiders carved out kingdoms from the territory of the waning western Roman Empire. To protect their estates, many local Roman landowners came to terms with the invaders, with the result that the successor kingdoms all acquired some important vestiges of Roman institutions and culture. ◆

SUCCESSOR KINGDOMS C. 500

——— Approximate frontiers of "barbarian" kingdoms c. 500

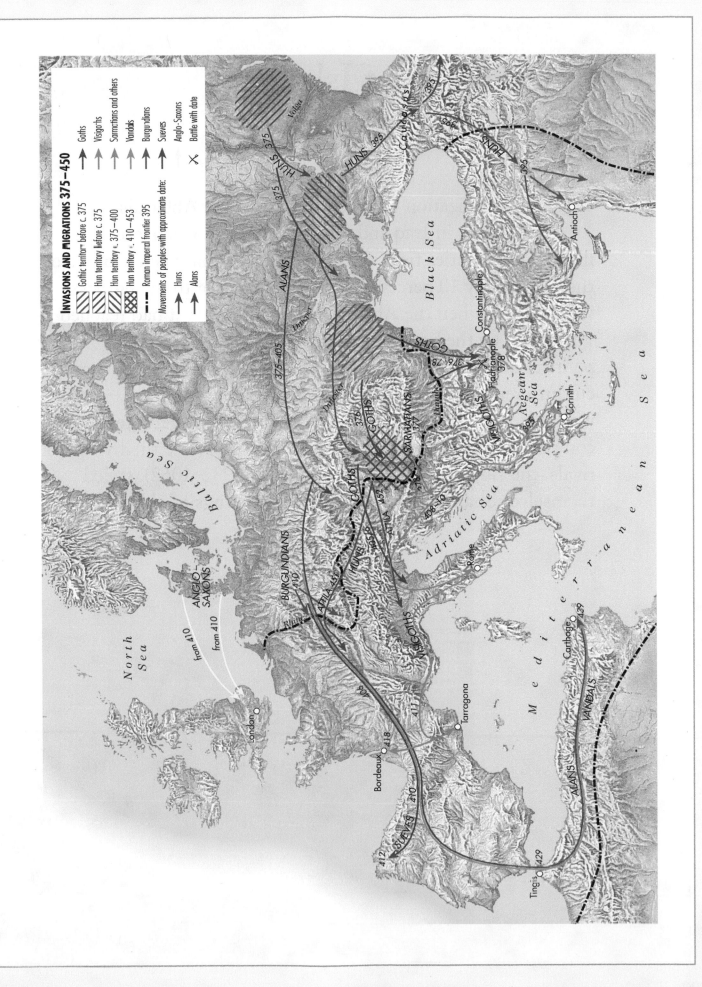

INVASIONS AND MIGRATIONS 375–450

Gothic territory before c. 375
Hun territory before c. 375
Hun territory c. 375–400
Hun territory c. 410–453
Roman imperial frontier 395

Movements of peoples with approximate date:

Goths
Visigoths
Sarmatians and others
Vandals
Burgundians
Sueves
Anglo-Saxons
Battle with date

Huns
Alans

North Sea

Baltic Sea

ANGLO-SAXONS

from 410

from 410

London

Volga

HUNS 375

HUNS 375

ALANS

Dnieper

375–405

Dniester

GOTHS 376

GOTHS

SARMATIANS 377

Danube

GOTHS

HUNS 451

ATTILA

ATTILA 452

BURGUNDIANS 410

Rhine

HUNS 451

ATTILA 451

Caucasus

395

395

HUNS

395

Black Sea

Constantinople

GOTHS

376/78

376/78

Adrianople 378

VISIGOTHS

395

Corinth

Aegean Sea

Antioch

408–10

VISIGOTHS

Rome

Adriatic Sea

Mediterranean Sea

Tarragona

Carthage 439

VANDALS

ALANS

SUEVES 410

Bordeaux 418

409

411

412

Tingis 429

31

15. The Spread of Islam

630–850 CE

✳ ✳ ✳

Rapid urbanization followed the rise of the Abbasids, particularly in Iraq and Persia, as would-be converts flocked to the cities from the countryside. It has been estimated that while only 10 percent of the population of these regions was Muslim when the Abbasids came to power, it had reached 90 percent by the beginning of the 10th century. As the political unity of the Muslim state began to disintegrate, local cultures reasserted themselves. The Samanid kings (819–1005) who ruled from their capital in Bukhara encouraged the composition of Persian poetry at their court, while their western rivals, the Buyid rulers of Iraq and Persia (932–1062), styled themselves Shahanshahs like the Persian kings of old.

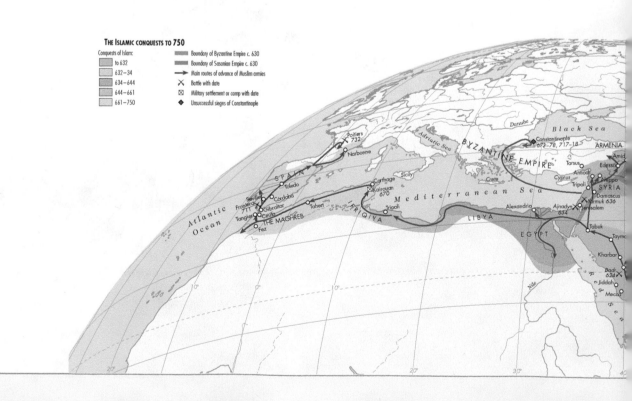

THE ISLAMIC CONQUESTS TO 750

Conquests of Islam:
- to 632
- 632–34
- 634–644
- 644–661
- 661–750

- Boundary of Byzantine Empire c. 630
- Boundary of Sasanian Empire c. 630
- → Main routes of advance of Muslim armies
- ✗ Battle with date
- ⊠ Military settlement or camp with date
- ◆ Unsuccessful sieges of Constantinople

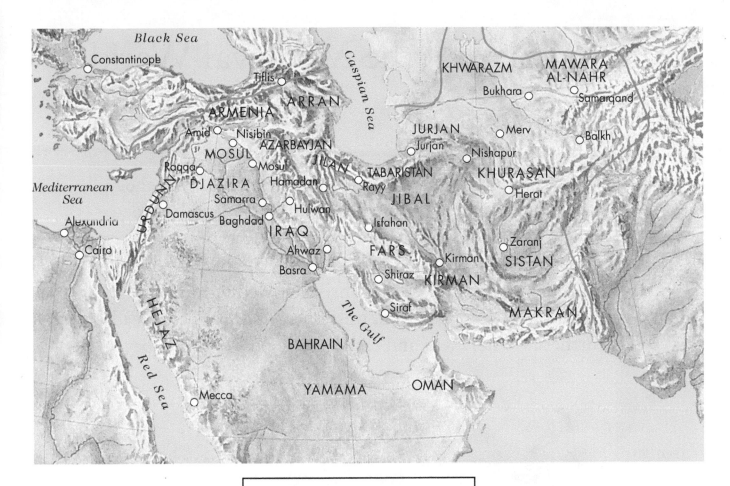

TERRITORIES CONTROLLED BY ABBASID CALIPHATE IN THE 9TH CENTURY

— Boundary of Abbasid Empire 850

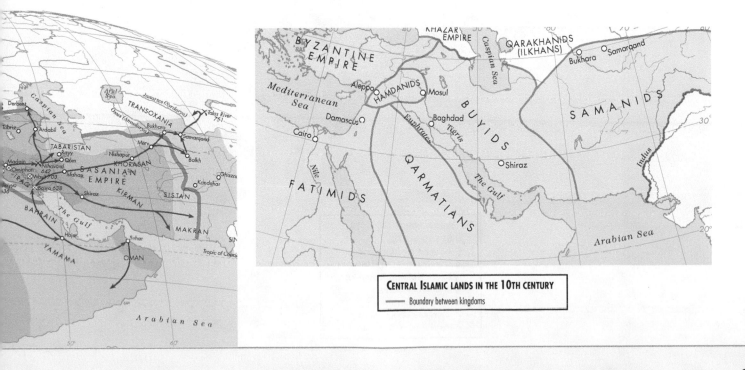

CENTRAL ISLAMIC LANDS IN THE 10TH CENTURY
— Boundary between kingdoms

16. Religions and the Medieval World
700–1450

✳ ✳ ✳

The last three centuries of the 1st millennium CE saw the steady development of a deep and lasting cultural divide between an eastern, Greek-rooted Orthodox tradition and a western, Latin-based Catholic culture. The rise of Islam from the 630s cut a swathe across the Christian Mediterranean world. By way of compensation, missionary Christianly spread ever further into northern and eastern Europe.

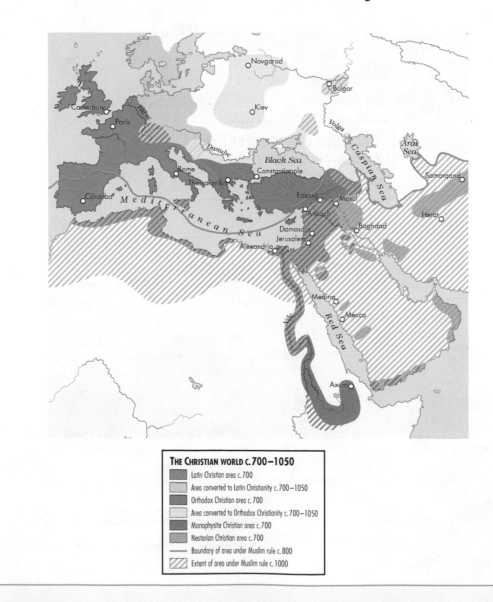

THE CHRISTIAN WORLD C. 700–1050

- Latin Christian area c. 700
- Area converted to Latin Christianity c. 700–1050
- Orthodox Christian area c. 700
- Area converted to Orthodox Christianity c. 700–1050
- Monophysite Christian area c. 700
- Nestorian Christian area c. 700
- Boundary of area under Muslim rule c. 800
- Extent of area under Muslim rule c. 1000

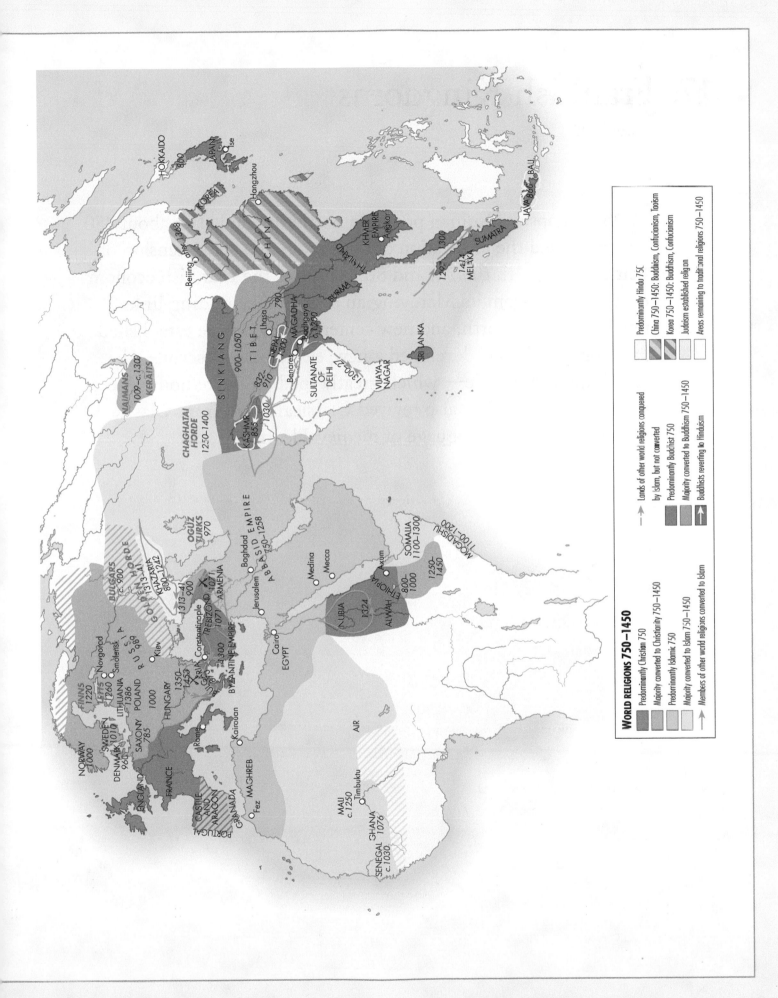

WORLD RELIGIONS 750–1450

- Predominantly Christian 750
- Majority converted to Christianity 750–1450
- Predominantly Islamic 750
- Majority converted to Islam 750–1450
- Members of other world religions converted to Islam
- → Lands of other world religions conquered by Islam, but not converted
- Predominantly Buddhist 750
- Majority converted to Buddhism 750–1450
- ⇑ Buddhists reverting to Hinduism
- Predominantly Hindu 750
- China 750–1450: Buddhism, Confucianism, Taoism
- Korea 750–1450: Buddhism, Confucianism
- Judaism established religion
- Areas remaining to traditional religions 750–1450

HOKKAIDO

KOREA

JAPAN · Ise
800

Beijing, after 1368

CHINA · Hangzhou

SINKIANG

NAIMANS
1009–c.1300

KERAITS

CHAGHATAI HORDE
1250–1400

TIBET · Lhasa
900–1050
832–910

NEPAL
1300

MAGADHA c.1200
Bodhgaya

Benares
SULTANATE OF DELHI
1300–27

KASHMIR
855
1030

THAILAND
790

BURMA

KHMER EMPIRE · Angkor

MELAKA
1414
1292–1300

SUMATRA

JAVA 865
BALI

VIJAYA NAGAR

SRI LANKA

SOMALIA
1100–1300

MOGADISHU
1100–1200

ETHIOPIA
800–1000
1250–1450

Axum

ALWAH

NUBIA
1324

EGYPT · Cairo

ABBASID EMPIRE 750–1258

Baghdad

Medina
Mecca

Jerusalem

OGUZ TURKS
970

KHAZARIA
800–1261

GOLDEN HORDE
1313–41

BULGARS
c.900

RUSSIA 989

Novgorod
Smolensk
1260

Kiev

ARMENIA
1071

TREBIZOND
1071

Constantinople

BYZANTINE EMPIRE

GREECE
1300
1350
1453

Rome

HUNGARY
1000

POLAND
1000

SAXONY
785

LITHUANIA
1386

LETTS
1260

FINNS
1220

SWEDEN
1010

NORWAY
1000

DENMARK
960

ENGLAND

FRANCE

PORTUGAL

CASTILE AND ARAGON

GRANADA

MAGHREB · Fez

Kairouan

AIR

MALI
c.1250 · Timbuktu

GHANA
1076

SENEGAL
c.1030

35

17. Frankish Kingdoms
482–800

* * *

The collapse of Roman power in northern Gaul after about 450 facilitated the unification of the Franks and the extension of their dominion. In the 7th and 8th centuries the Frankish economy recovered well from its Merovingian decline. Sea trading links flourished to the north, and new centers of trade were established. Carolingian scholars developed a new, easily written script—the Carolingian miniscule— which greatly sped up the tedious process of book copying. They also revived Classical Latin from Classical texts, making it the language of medieval learning.

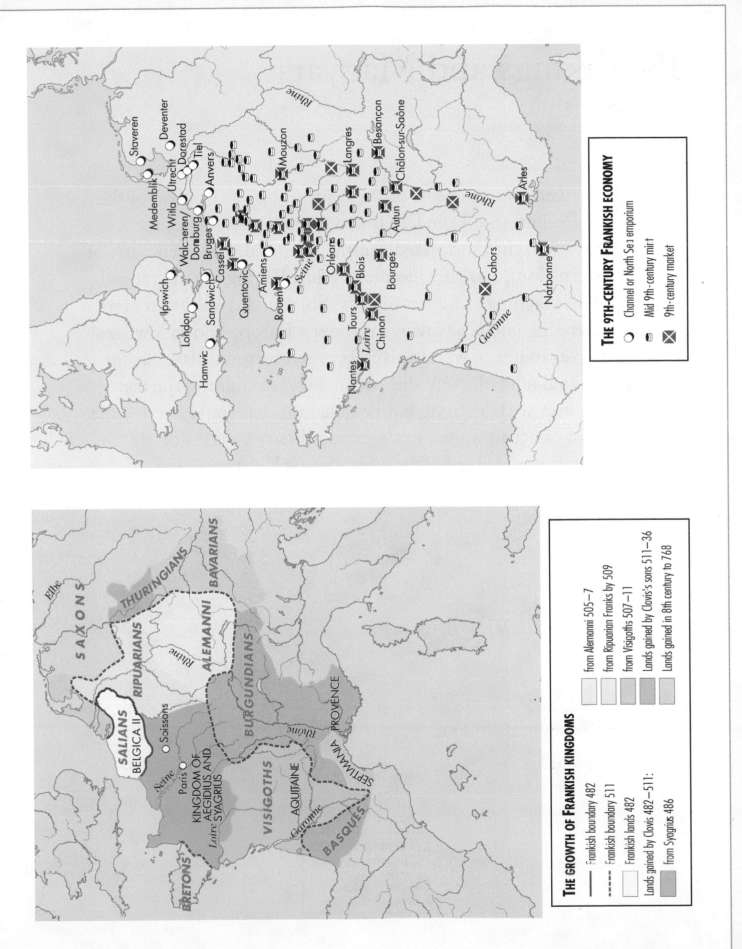

THE 9TH-CENTURY FRANKISH ECONOMY

Rhine

Staveren
Deventer
Dorestad
Medemblik
Utrecht
Witla
Tiel
Walcheren/
Domburg
Anvers
Bruges
Cassel

Ipswich
London
Sandwich
Quentovic
Hamwic

Mouzon
Langres
Besançon
Châlon-sur-Saône

Amiens
Rouen
Seine
Orléans
Blois
Bourges
Autun

Tours
Chinon
Loire
Nantes

Arles
Rhône

Cahors

Narbonne
Garonne

○ Channel or North Sea emporium

◐ Mid 9th-century mint

⊠ 9th-century market

THE GROWTH OF FRANKISH KINGDOMS

Elbe

SAXONS
THURINGIANS
RIPUARIANS
BAVARIANS
ALEMANNI
Rhine

SALIANS
BELGICA II
○ Soissons
KINGDOM OF
AEGIDIUS AND
SYAGRIUS
Seine
● Paris
Loire
BURGUNDIANS
Rhône
PROVENCE

VISIGOTHS
AQUITAINE
SEPTIMANIA
Garonne
BASQUES

BRETONS

— Frankish boundary 482

- - - Frankish boundary 511

☐ Frankish lands 482

Lands gained by Clovis 482–511:

▨ from Syagrius 486

☐ from Alemanni 505–7

☐ from Ripuarian Franks by 509

☐ from Visigoths 507–11

☐ Lands gained by Clovis's sons 511–36

☐ Lands gained in 8th century to 768

18. Vikings and Magyars
800–1100

* * *

Driven into the heart of the continent by the arrival of the Pechenegs on the Ukrainian steppe around 895, the Magyars in turn terrorized central, southern, and even parts of western Europe with widespread raids. Viking raiders ranged widely, reaching the coast of Italy. So, too, did Viking traders, exchanging goods at towns in western Europe and following the river routes of western Russia to sell furs and slaves as far away as Baghdad. New ship technology, combining the use of sail power with a strong but flexible hull that could survive the impact of ocean waves, made extraordinary voyages of exploration possible for the adventurous Vikings.

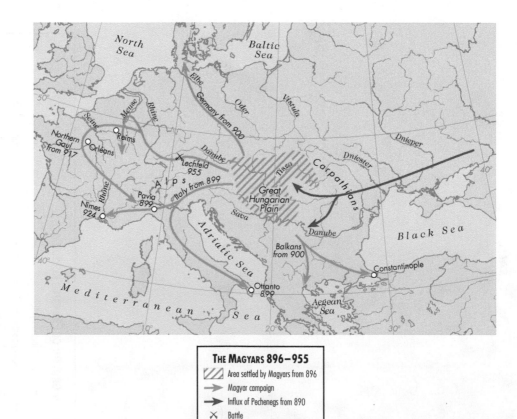

THE MAGYARS 896–955

▨ Area settled by Magyars from 896

→ Magyar campaign

➜ Influx of Pechenegs from 890

✕ Battle

19. The Muslim World

1000—1200

* * *

During the 10th century the political unity of the Muslim world collapsed. The Abbasid caliphs, previously dominant from the Atlantic to India, were replaced by a series of regional dynasties, and the caliph in Baghdad was reduced to little more than a religious figurehead. Under Malik Shah, the Seljuk-led warbands of the Oguz Turks reunited much of the old Abbasid Empire. The unity fostered by the Seljuks in the 11th century was illusory. In the 12th century the Muslim world fragmented into a series of regional authorities—a localization of power which made possible gains by the Byzantines, crusaders, nomads, and others at the expense of particular Muslim communities.

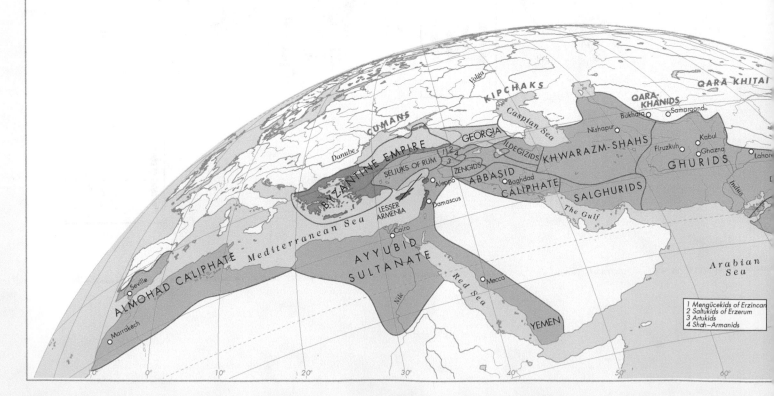

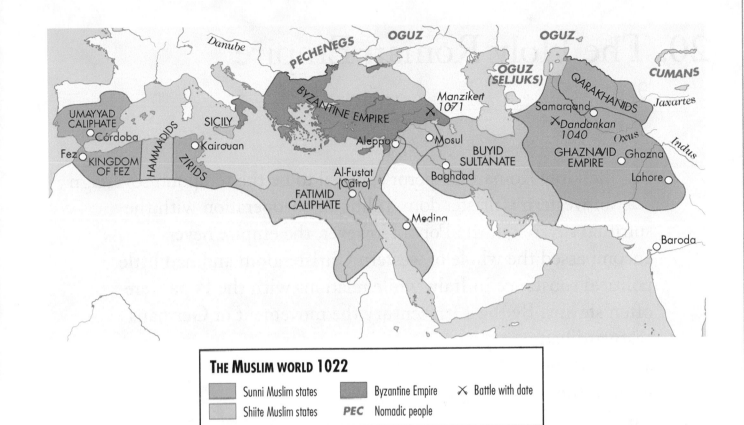

THE MUSLIM WORLD 1022

▦ Sunni Muslim states	▦ Byzantine Empire
▦ Shiite Muslim states	**PEC** Nomadic people
✕ Battle with date	

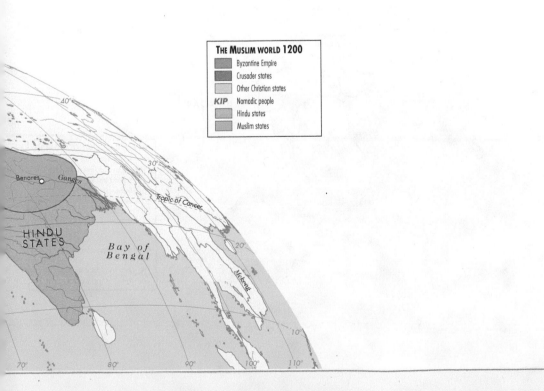

THE MUSLIM WORLD 1200

▦ Byzantine Empire
▦ Crusader states
▦ Other Christian states
KIP Nomadic people
▦ Hindu states
▦ Muslim states

20. The Holy Roman Empire
950–1360

* * *

The Holy Roman Emperor claimed to be the temporal sovereign of western Christendom, ruling in co-operation with the spiritual sovereign, the Pope. However, the empire never encompassed the whole of western Christendom and had little political substance in Italy, while relations with the Pope were often stormy. By the 13th century the movement of Germans eastward had advanced the limit of the Empire eastward.

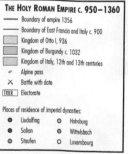

THE HOLY ROMAN EMPIRE c. 950–1360
- —— Boundary of empire 1356
- —— Boundary of East Francia and Italy c. 900
- Kingdom of Otto I, 936
- Kingdom of Burgundy c. 1032
- Kingdom of Italy, 12th and 13th centuries
- ⌁ Alpine pass
- ✕ Battle with date
- TRIER Electorate

Places of residence of imperial dynasties:
- ● Liudolfing
- ○ Habsburg
- ● Salian
- ○ Wittelsbach
- ● Staufen
- ○ Luxembourg

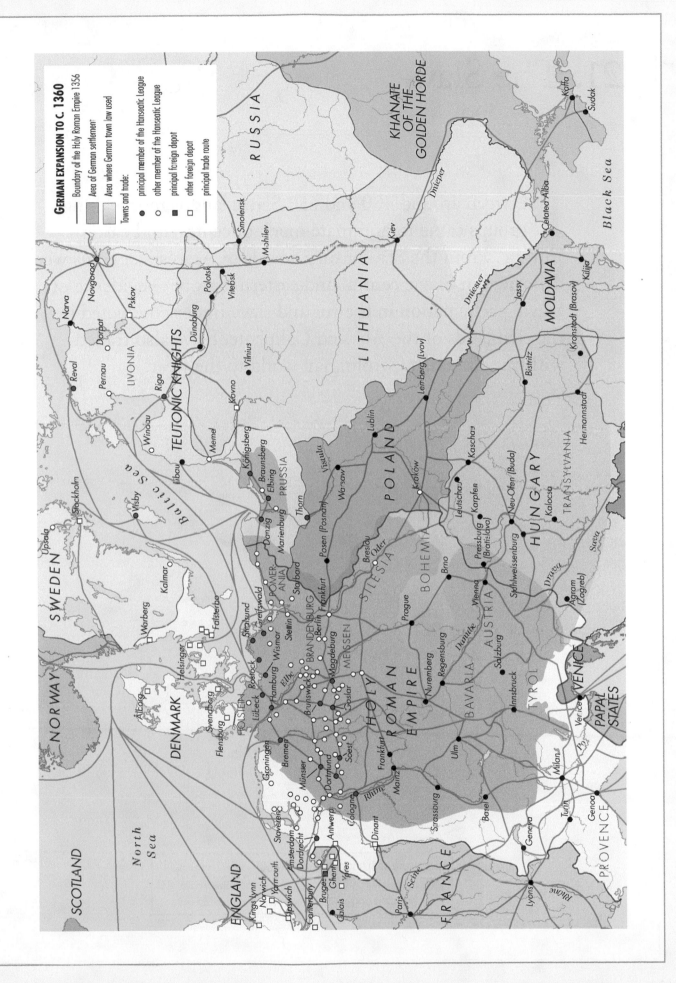

GERMAN EXPANSION TO C. 1360

Boundary of the Holy Roman Empire 1356

Area of German settlement

Area where German town law used

Towns and trade:

● principal member of the Hanseatic League

○ other member of the Hanseatic League

■ principal foreign depot

□ other foreign depot

principal trade route

SCOTLAND

ENGLAND

Kings Lynn

Norwich

Yarmouth

Ipswich

Canterbury

Calais

North Sea

NORWAY

SWEDEN

Upsala

Stockholm

Kalmar

Alborg

Warberg

Helsingor

Falsterbo

Svendborg

Flensburg

DENMARK

HOLSTEIN

Lübeck

Hamburg

Wismar

Rostock

Groningen

Staveren

Amsterdam

Dordrecht

Bremen

Münster

Dortmund

Soest

Cologne

Antwerp

Ghent

Bruges

Ypres

Dinant

Frankfurt

Mainz

Strassburg

Basel

Paris

Seine

Rhine

FRANCE

Rhône

Lyons

Geneva

PROVENCE

Turin

Milan

Genoa

Venice

VENICE

Po

PAPAL STATES

Innsbruck

TYROL

Salzburg

BAVARIA

Ulm

Regensburg

Nuremberg

Prague

BOHEMIA

Brno

AUSTRIA

Vienna

Danube

HOLY ROMAN EMPIRE

MEISSEN

Magdeburg

Goslar

Brunswick

Berlin

Frankfurt

BRANDENBURG

Elbe

Stettin

Greifswald

Stralsund

POMER- ANIA

Stolpard

Danzig

Marienburg

Thorn

Elbing

Braunsberg

Königsberg

Memel

PRUSSIA

TEUTONIC KNIGHTS

Visula

Posen (Posnan)

Breslau

Oder

SILESIA

POLAND

Warsaw

Kraków

Lublin

Lemberg (Lvov)

Baltic Sea

Visby

Libau

Riga

Winqu

Pernau

Dünaburg

Dorpat

LIVONIA

Reval

Narva

Pskov

Novgorod

Smolensk

Polotsk

Vitebsk

Mohilev

RUSSIA

LITHUANIA

Vilnius

Kovno

Kiev

Dnieper

Dniester

Dniester

KHANATE OF THE GOLDEN HORDE

Kaffa

Sudak

Cetatea Alba

Kilija

Black Sea

MOLDAVIA

Jassy

Bistritz

Kronstadt (Brasov)

Hermannstadt

TRANSYLVANIA

Agram (Zagreb)

Drava

Sava

Kalocsa

Stahlweissenburg

HUNGARY

Neu-Ofen (Buda)

Karpfen

Leutschau

Kaschau

Pressburg (Bratislava)

43

21. The Slavs

300–1000

✳ ✳ ✳

Between around 400 and 650 Slavic language–speaking groups came to dominate much of central and eastern Europe. From the 8th century hoards of Arab silver coins were deposited in Slavic central and eastern Europe—evidence of Slavic participation in the fur and slave trades conducted in the rich lands of the Abbasid Caliphate. Slavs also traded with the Frankish Carolingian world to the west.

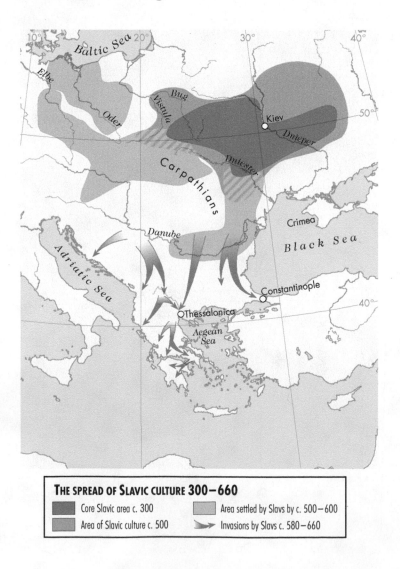

THE SPREAD OF SLAVIC CULTURE 300–660

- Core Slavic area c. 300
- Area of Slavic culture c. 500
- Area settled by Slavs by c. 500–600
- Invasions by Slavs c. 580–660

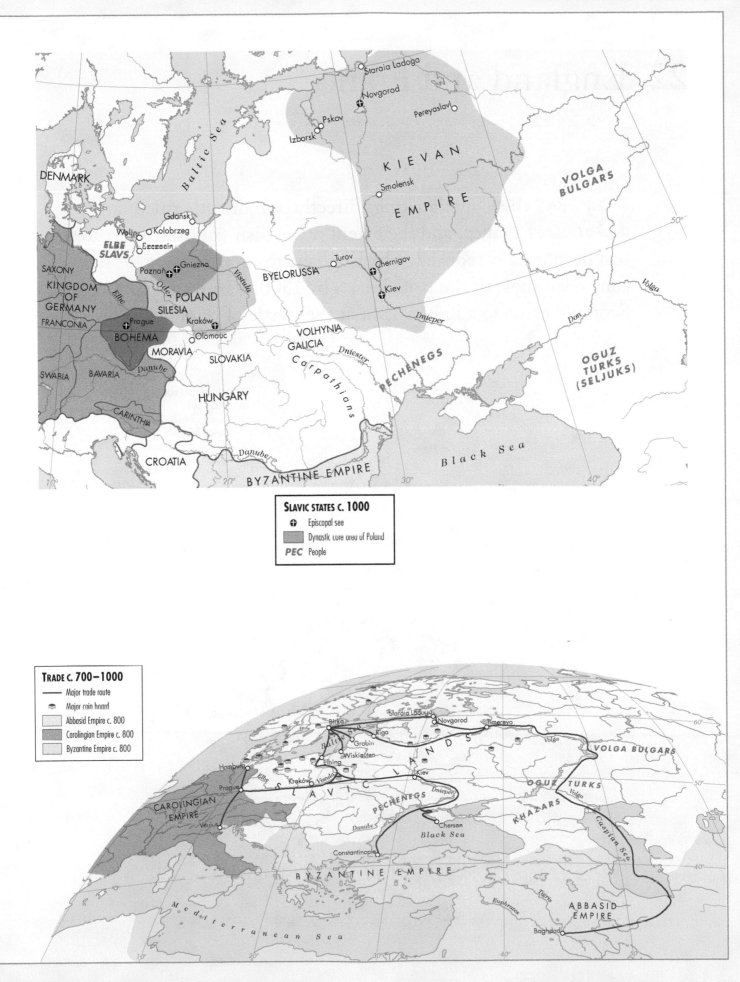

SLAVIC STATES C. 1000

✠   Episcopal see

    Dynastic core area of Poland

PEC   People

Map labels (upper map):

DENMARK · Baltic Sea · Staraia Ladoga · Novgorod · Pskov · Pereyaslavl · Izborsk · KIEVAN · VOLGA BULGARS · Gdańsk · Wolin · Kolobrzeg · ELBE SLAVS · Szczecin · Smolensk · EMPIRE · SAXONY · Poznań · Gniezno · Vistula · BYELORUSSIA · Turov · Chernigov · KINGDOM OF GERMANY · Oder · POLAND · Elbe · SILESIA · Kiev · Volga · FRANCONIA · Prague · Kraków · BOHEMA · Olomouc · VOLHYNIA · Dnieper · Don · MORAVIA · GALICIA · Dniester · OGUZ TURKS (SELJUKS) · SWABIA · BAVARIA · Danube · SLOVAKIA · Carpathians · PECHENEGS · CARINTHIA · HUNGARY · CROATIA · Danube · BYZANTINE EMPIRE · Black Sea

TRADE C. 700–1000

—   Major trade route

    Major coin hoard

    Abbasid Empire c. 800

    Carolingian Empire c. 800

    Byzantine Empire c. 800

Map labels (lower map):

Birka · Staraia Ladoga · Novgorod · Timerevo · Riga · VOLGA BULGARS · Baltic Sea · Grobin · Volga · Wiskiauten · Hamburg · Elbing · SLAVIC LANDS · OGUZ TURKS · Elbe · Kraków · Vistula · Kiev · Volga · Prague · Dnieper · KHAZARS · CAROLINGIAN EMPIRE · PECHENEGS · Caspian Sea · Venice · Danube · Cherson · Black Sea · Constantinople · BYZANTINE EMPIRE · Tigris · ABBASID EMPIRE · Mediterranean Sea · Euphrates · Baghdad

22. England and France

1265–1295

* * *

By 1265 the Capetian kings directly or indirectly ruled large areas of France, and the extent of English-controlled territory had been greatly reduced. The English crown effectively controlled most of the British Isles by 1300. Its advance into Scotland came to a halt in 1314 at the Battle of Bannockburn.

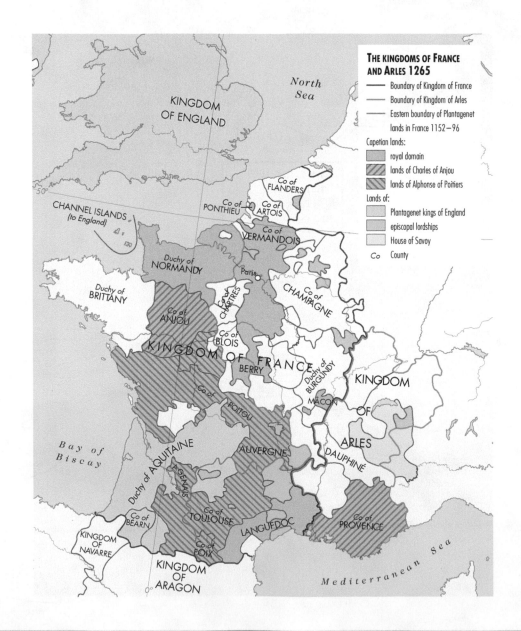

THE KINGDOMS OF FRANCE AND ARLES 1265

— Boundary of Kingdom of France
— Boundary of Kingdom of Arles
— Eastern boundary of Plantagenet lands in France 1152–96

Capetian lands:
- royal domain
- lands of Charles of Anjou
- lands of Alphonse of Poitiers

Lands of:
- Plantagenet kings of England
- episcopal lordships
- House of Savoy

Co   County

ENGLISH LANDS 1295

Area controlled by English kings

Area under Marcher Lordships

Irish districts outside the limits of royal authority

Kingdom of Scotland

Norwegian territory

Major castle

Battle with date

to Norway

Inverness

Kingdom of
SCOTLAND

Aberdeen

Dunkeld

Perth

St Andrews

to Scotland from Norway 1266

Stirling

Bannockburn 1314

Glasgow

Edinburgh

Berwick

Newcastle

Carlisle

Richmond

Carrickfergus

THE GREAT IRISHRY

Skipton

York

Grimsby

Trim

Dublin

Beaumaris

Rhuddlan

Conwy

Flint

Chester

Boston

Criccieth

Harlech

Limerick

Shrewsbury

Leicester

Norwich

Aberystwyth

Northampton

Cambridge

Waterford

Carmarthen

Hereford

Pembroke

Oxford

Cardiff

Bristol

Bath

London

Winchester

Dover

Southampton

Exeter

23. The Mediterranean

1100–1300

* * *

The era of the Crusades was also one of growing Mediterranean commerce. European traders took some textiles and foodstuffs east, but above all they carried silver coins with which to purchase the valuable dyes and spices that came from India and the Far East.

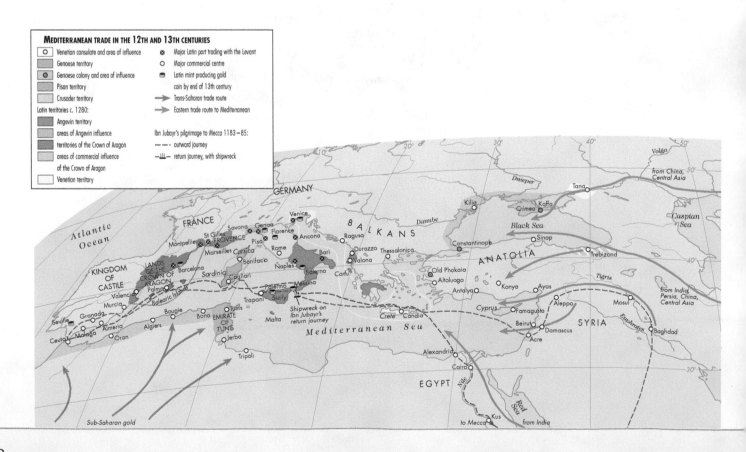

MEDITERRANEAN TRADE IN THE 12TH AND 13TH CENTURIES

- ○ Venetian consulate and area of influence
- Genoese territory
- ◉ Genoese colony and area of influence
- Pisan territory
- Crusader territory

Latin territories c. 1280:
- Angevin territory
- areas of Angevin influence
- territories of the Crown of Aragon
- areas of commercial influence of the Crown of Aragon
- Venetian territory

- ⊗ Major Latin port trading with the Levant
- ○ Major commercial centre
- ⬭ Latin mint producing gold coin by end of 13th century
- → Trans-Saharan trade route
- → Eastern trade route to Mediterranean

Ibn Jubayr's pilgrimage to Mecca 1183–85:
- – – – outward journey
- –⣿⣿– return journey, with shipwreck

Meanwhile, in Spain, Christian kings strengthened their position by organizing opposition to the Muslim rulers in the south. Having held out against the Almohads and Almoravids, they overran much of the Muslim territory in the 13th century.

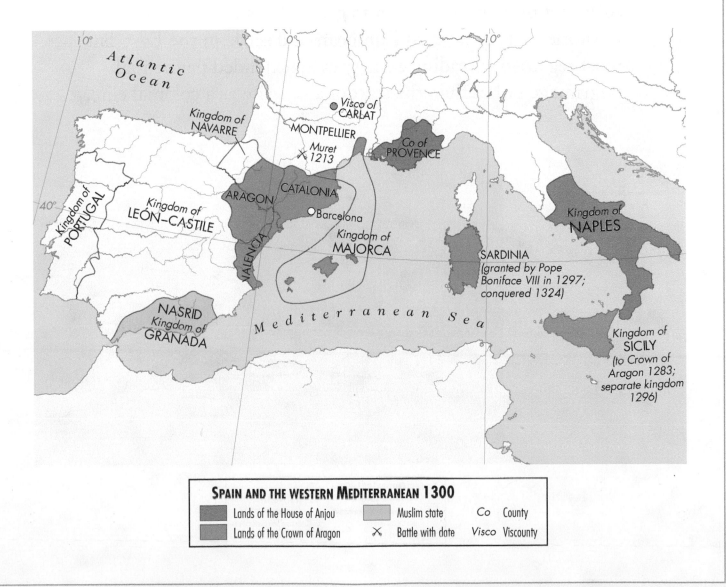

SPAIN AND THE WESTERN MEDITERRANEAN 1300

▨ Lands of the House of Anjou	▨ Muslim state	*Co* County
▨ Lands of the Crown of Aragon	✕ Battle with date	*Visco* Viscounty

24. The World of the Crusaders

1095–1140

✳ ✳ ✳

The backbone of the armies of the First Crusade was provided by knights traveling as part of their lords' households. The capture of Jerusalem in July 1099 after two years of journeying—and a series of unlikely military victories—convinced survivors and contemporaries that the enterprise had been blessed by God. Despite many appeals, the Christian rulers of the Crusader states were unable to attract sufficient military manpower to ensure the survival of their territories. Many western Europeans did settle in the East, but most regarded crusading activity as an extended penitential pilgrimage rather than the start of a new life as a colonial elite.

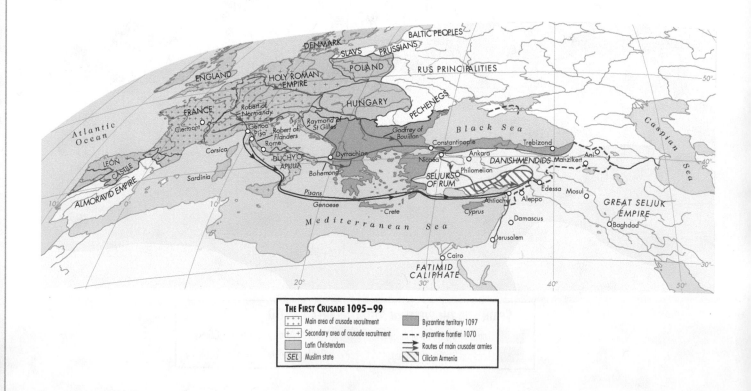

THE FIRST CRUSADE 1095–99

┼┼┼ Main area of crusade recruitment	Byzantine territory 1097
┼ ┼ Secondary area of crusade recruitment	– – – Byzantine frontier 1070
Latin Christendom	Routes of main crusader armies
SEL Muslim state	Cilician Armenia

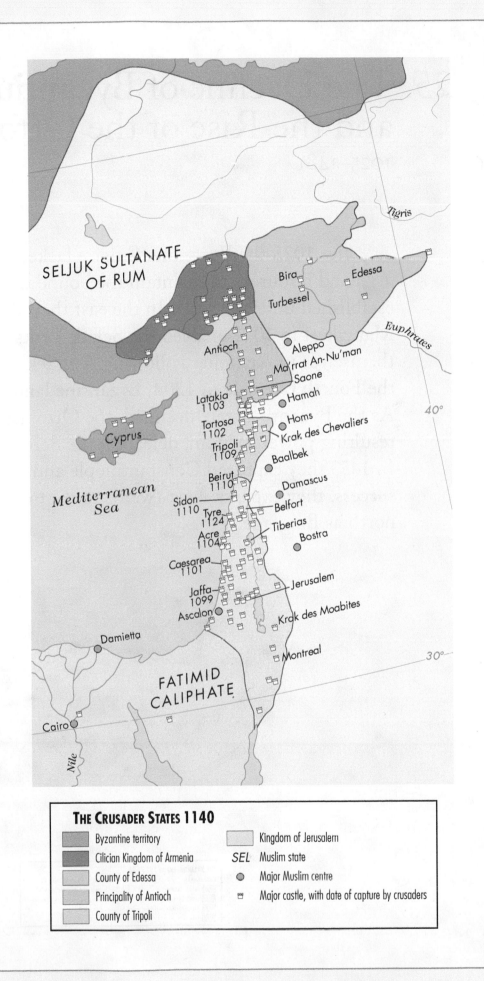

Tigris

SELJUK SULTANATE
OF RUM

Bira

Edessa

Turbessel

Euphrates

Antioch

Aleppo

Ma'rrat An-Nu'man

Saone

Latakia
1103

Hamah

Tortosa
1102

Homs

Krak des Chevaliers

Tripoli
1109

Baalbek

Cyprus

Beirut
1110

Damascus

Sidon
1110

Belfort

*Mediterranean
Sea*

Tyre
1124

Tiberias

Acre
1104

Bostra

Caesarea
1101

Jaffa
1099

Jerusalem

Ascalon

Krak des Moabites

Damietta

Montreal

40°

30°

FATIMID
CALIPHATE

Cairo

Nile

THE CRUSADER STATES 1140

	Byzantine territory		Kingdom of Jerusalem
	Cilician Kingdom of Armenia	*SEL*	Muslim state
	County of Edessa	●	Major Muslim centre
	Principality of Antioch	⌂	Major castle, with date of capture by crusaders
	County of Tripoli		

51

25. The Decline of Byzantium and the Rise of the Ottomans
1025–1481

❋ ❋ ❋

After 1025 the Byzantine Empire lacked the infrastructure and resources to maintain the boundaries that had been established under Basil II. In the east their defeat in the Battle of Manzikert in 1071 enabled the Seljuk Turks to establish themselves in Anatolia. Following the sack of Constantinople by the Fourth Crusade in 1204, Byzantine lands were divided up. As the Byzantine state declined, the Ottomans moved in to fill the resulting power vacuum, defeating the Serbs in Kosovo in 1389. In 1453 they captured Constantinople and, strengthened by this success, they expanded westwards to control the Balkans as far north as Belgrade.

THE BYZANTINE EMPIRE 1025–96

Dominant religion:

- Orthodox Christianity
- Catholic Christianity
- Monophysite and other Christian traditions
- Islam

—— Boundary of Byzantine Empire 1025
- Territory under Byzantine control 1096
- Territory taken by Seljuks of Rum 1072–96
✕ Battle with date

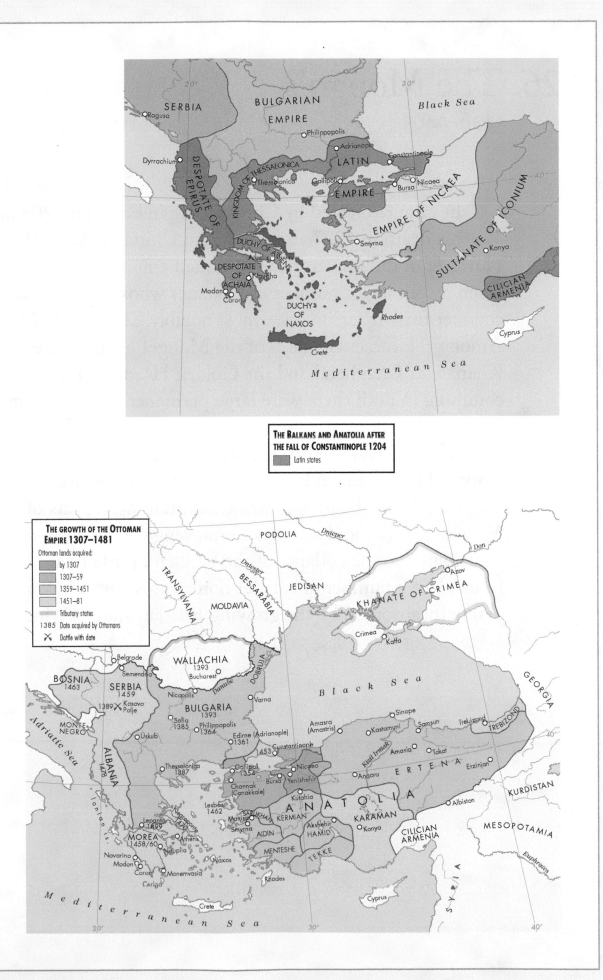

26. The Mongols
1206–1405

* * *

The empire created by Chinggis Khan between 1206 and his death in 1227 stretched from China to Persia (Iran). However, it did not survive as a united empire beyond 1260 when it split into a number of khanates whose rulers went on to conquer further territories—most notably China in 1279. Among the successor states of the Mongol Empire, the Khanate of Chaghatai and the Golden Horde had much in common: in both there were large permanently settled areas controlled by nomads living on the steppe. The relatively small number of Mongols, both elite and commoners, were gradually absorbed by the much larger Turkish tribal population, adopting Turkic languages while maintaining aspects of Mongol identity and culture. Timur-leng's campaigns contributed to the collapse of the Golden Horde around 1400. In its place a number of smaller hordes arose, which were gradually absorbed by the growing Russian state of Muscovy.

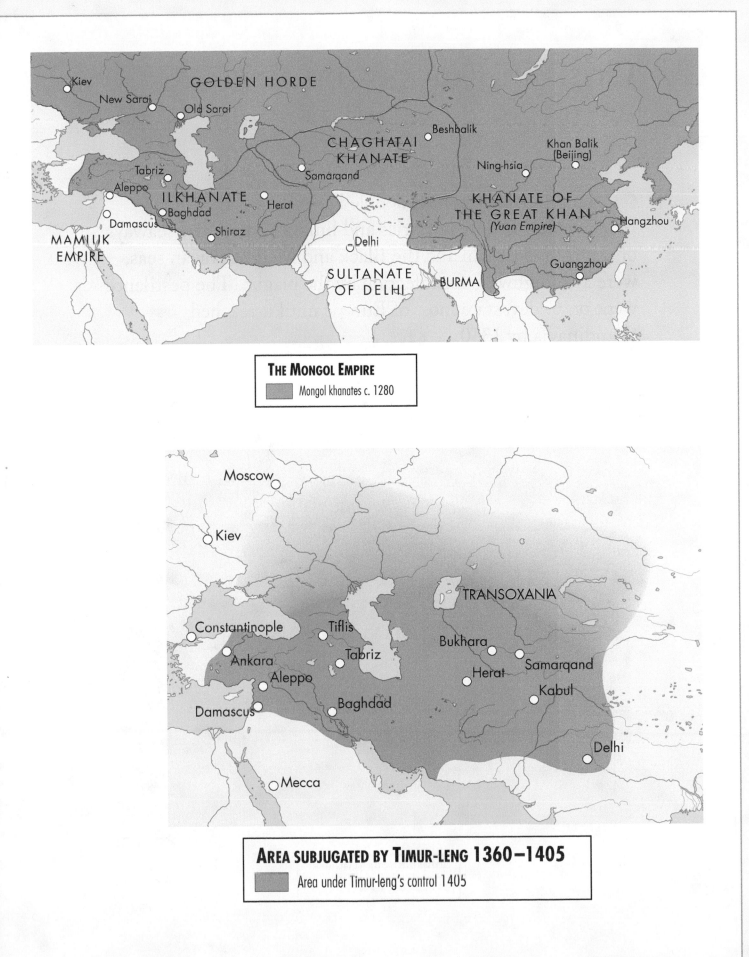

THE MONGOL EMPIRE

Mongol khanates c. 1280

Kiev · New Sarai · Old Sarai · GOLDEN HORDE · Beshbalik · CHAGHATAI KHANATE · Khan Balik (Beijing) · Ning-hsia · Tabriz · Samarqand · Aleppo · ILKHANATE · Herat · KHANATE OF THE GREAT KHAN (Yuan Empire) · Baghdad · Hangzhou · Damascus · Shiraz · MAMLUK EMPIRE · Delhi · Guangzhou · SULTANATE OF DELHI · BURMA

AREA SUBJUGATED BY TIMUR-LENG 1360–1405

Area under Timur-leng's control 1405

Moscow · Kiev · TRANSOXANIA · Constantinople · Tiflis · Bukhara · Ankara · Tabriz · Herat · Samarqand · Aleppo · Kabul · Baghdad · Damascus · Delhi · Mecca

27. Crisis in Europe and Asia

1330–1352

✳ ✳ ✳

The Silk Roads, which doubled as military routes for invaders and mercenaries and linked up with the seaways of the Indian Ocean and the Black and Mediterranean seas, were also highways for infection by the plague. The pestilence went on to devastate most of Europe until it reached Scandinavia by 1350.

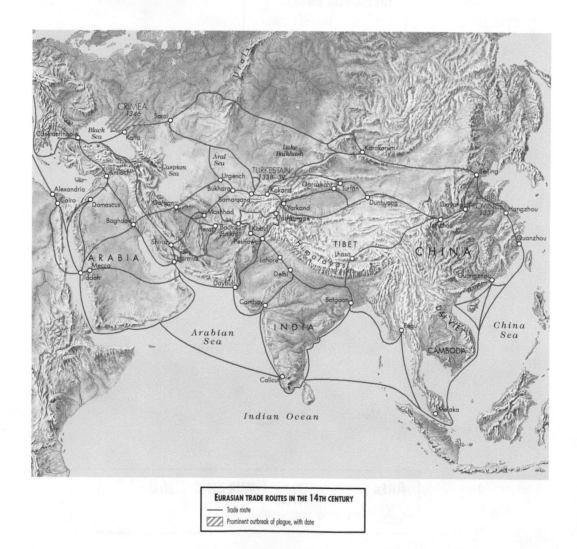

EURASIAN TRADE ROUTES IN THE 14TH CENTURY
— Trade route
▨ Prominent outbreak of plague, with date

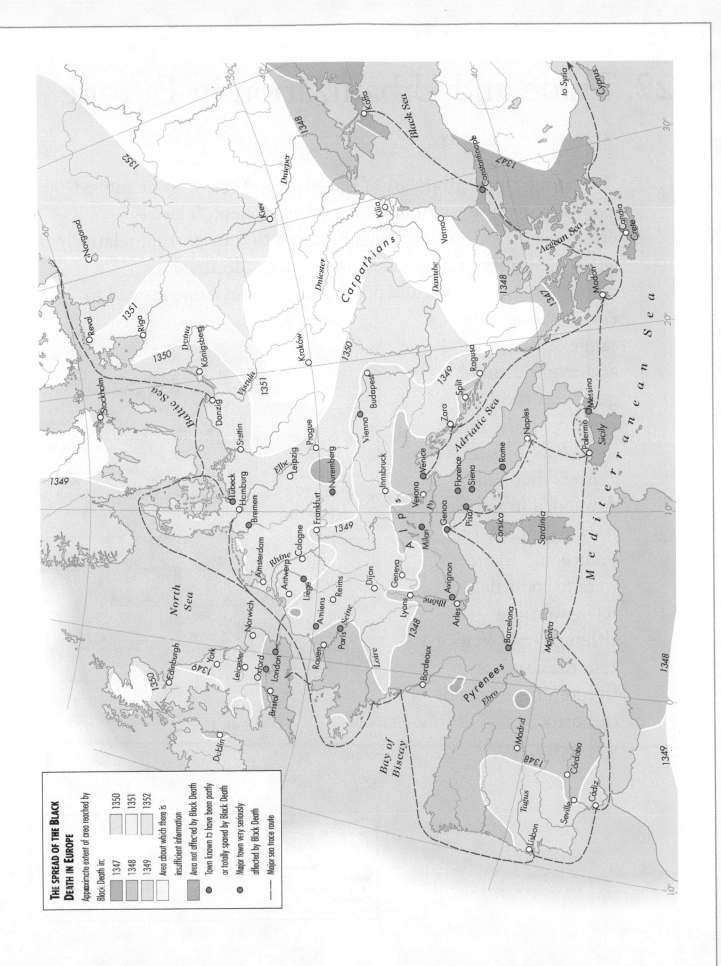

THE SPREAD OF THE BLACK DEATH IN EUROPE

Approximate extent of area reached by Black Death in:

1347
1348
1349
1350
1351
1352

Area about which there is insufficient information

Area not affected by Black Death

● Town known to have been partly or totally spared by Black Death

● Major town very seriously affected by Black Death

— Major sea trace route

Novgorod

Reval
Riga
1351
1350
Deina
Königsberg

Stockholm
Danzig
Stettin
1351
Vistula

Lübeck
Hamburg
Bremen
Elbe
Leipzig
Prague
Nuremberg
1349

Amsterdam
Antwerp
Cologne
Frankfurt
Rhine
Liège
Reims
Dijon
Amiens
Seine
Paris
Rouen
Loire

Norwich
Edinburgh
York
Leicester
Oxford
London
Bristol
Dublin
1350
1349

North Sea

Baltic Sea

Kiev
Dnieper

1352

1348

Kilia
Dniester
Kraków
1350

Budapest
Vienna
1351
Innsbruck

Carpathians

Danube

Varna

Black Sea

to Syria
Cyprus

Constantinople
1347

Aegean Sea

Candia
Crete

Modon

Mediterranean Sea

1348
1347
1349

Ragusa
Split
Zara
Venice
Verona
Po
Genoa
Pisa
Florence
Siena
Rome
Milan
Geneva
Lyons
Avignon
Rhône
Arles
1348

Adriatic Sea

Alps

Naples
Messina
Palermo
Sicily

Corsica
Sardinia

Barcelona
Majorca
1348

Bay of Biscay

Bordeaux
Pyrenees
Ebro

Madrid
1348
Tagus
Córdoba
Seville
Cádiz
1349
Lisbon

40
30
20
10
0

57

28. Trade and Urbanization in Europe

＊＊＊

During the central part of the Middle Ages, Europe moved decisively away from locally self-sufficient, "closed" economies. Trade was no longer limited to transporting relatively small quantities of high-value luxury items destined for consumption by a rich and privileged elite but came instead to encompass a wide range of agricultural and manufactured goods. In the 14th century all the towns in the two urban clusters that had developed in northern Italy and northern France and Flanders were to some degree self-governing, although only Venice asserted absolute freedom from outside authority.

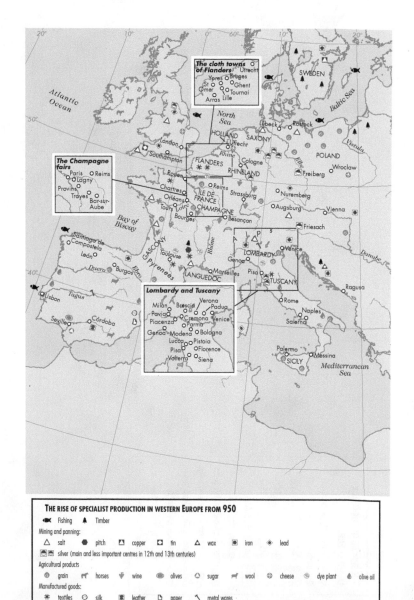

THE RISE OF SPECIALIST PRODUCTION IN WESTERN EUROPE FROM 950

⬛ Fishing   ▲ Timber

Mining and panning:

△ salt   ● pitch   ◰ copper   ◱ tin   △ wax   ◉ iron   ◉ lead

◨◧ silver (main and less important centres in 12th and 13th centuries)

Agricultural products

◉ grain   🐎 horses   ▼ wine   ◉ olives   ○ sugar   🐑 wool   ◎ cheese   ◉ dye plant   ◉ olive oil

Manufactured goods:

＊ textiles   ○ silk   ▣ leather   ▯ paper   ＼ metal wares

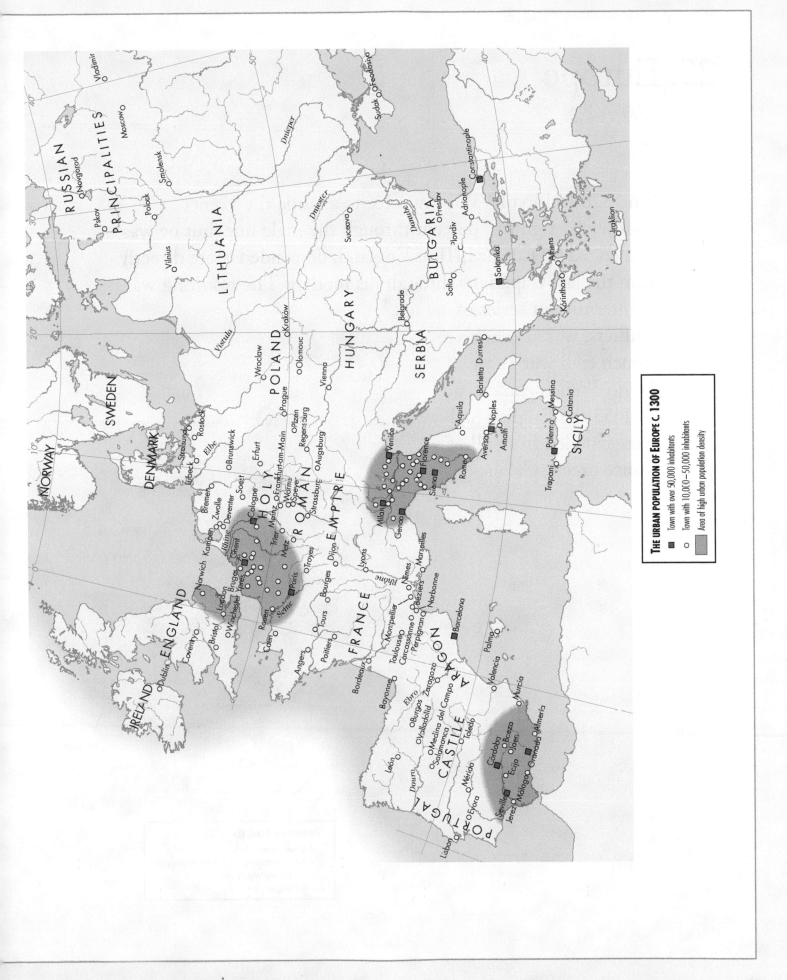

29. Europe

1350–1453

✳ ✳ ✳

In 1328 Philip of Valois was able to assume the French crown by rights of descent through the male line, but he was challenged by Edward III of England, descended more directly from the last Capetians through his mother. The resulting war, an intermittent series of conflicts, was as much a French civil war as an Anglo-French contest. By 1453 the English had been expelled from all of France except Calais.

THE HUNDRED YEARS WAR 1337–1453

▉ Plantagenet territory c. 1300

▢ Plantagenet territory recognized by the Treaty of Brétigny 1360

▨ Area recognizing Plantagenet kingship 1420–28

✕ Major battle with date

The initial cause of the Great Schism was a disputed papal election in 1378. It lasted for almost forty years (1378–1417) because lay political groups exploited the situation, rapidly aligning themselves behind the rival claimants to papal office.

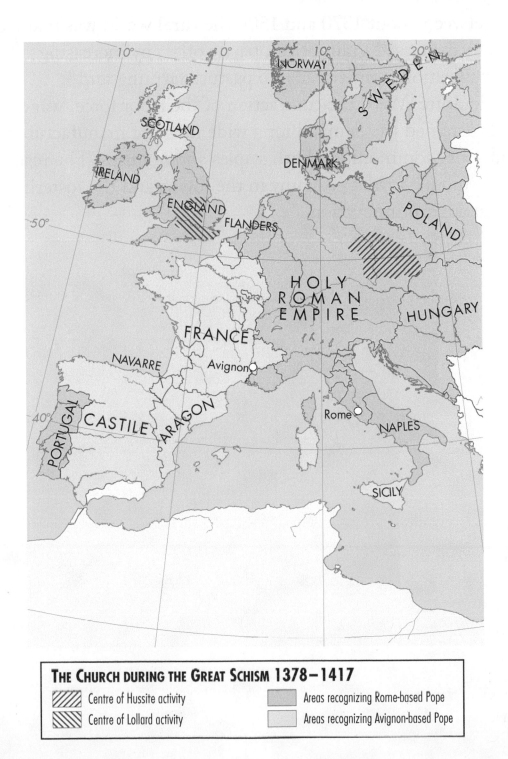

THE CHURCH DURING THE GREAT SCHISM 1378–1417

Centre of Hussite activity	Areas recognizing Rome-based Pope
Centre of Lollard activity	Areas recognizing Avignon-based Pope

30. The European Economy in the 15th Century

* * *

Between about 1370 and 1500 the rural world was marked by depressed grain prices, partly offset by increasing diversification from arable into pasture farming and horticulture. With the contraction of the labor force, wages rose and sustained the demand for a wide range of manufactured and other commodities, both staples and luxuries. The result was a more buoyant economy in the towns and the fostering of technological innovation.

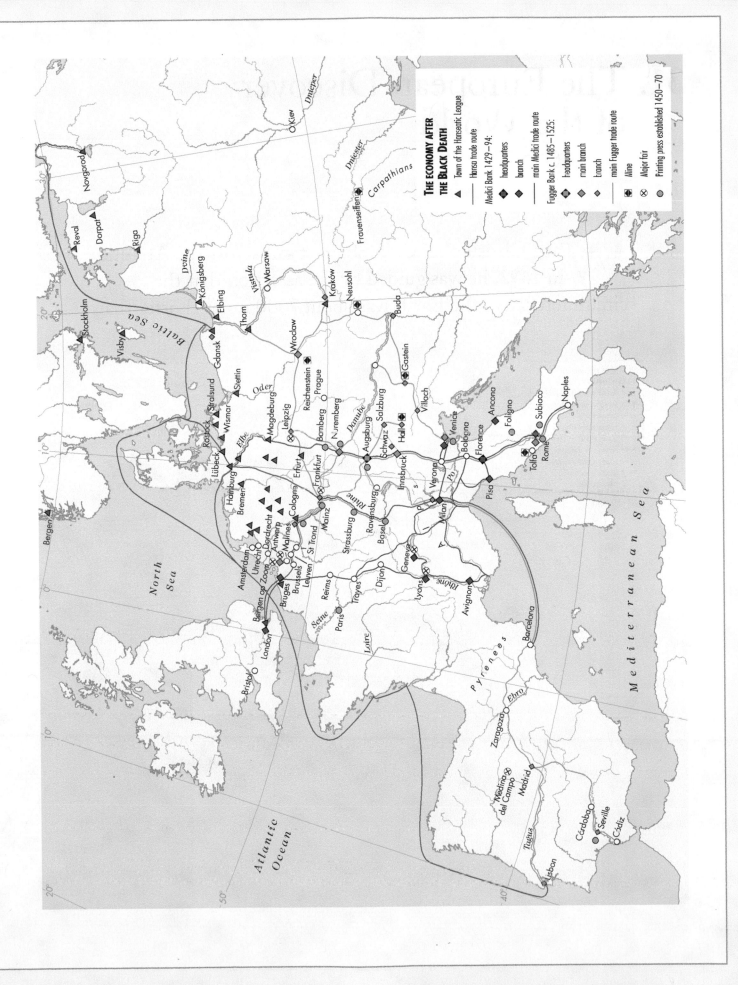

THE ECONOMY AFTER THE BLACK DEATH

- ▲ Town of the Hanseatic League
- —— Hansa trade route

Medici Bank 1429–94:
- ◆ headquarters
- ◆ branch
- —— main Medici trade route

Fugger Bank c. 1485–1525:
- ◆ headquarters
- ◆ main branch
- ◆ branch
- —— main Fugger trade route
- ◈ Mine
- ⊗ Major fair
- ● Printing press established 1450–70

North Sea

Baltic Sea

Atlantic Ocean

Mediterranean Sea

Novgorod
Reval
Dorpat
Riga
Stockholm
Visby
Bergen
Königsberg
Elbing
Warsaw
Thorn
Kraków
Neusohl
Buda
Gdańsk
Stettin
Stralsund
Rostock
Wismar
Lübeck
Hamburg
Bremen
Magdeburg
Leipzig
Wrocław
Reichenstein
Prague
Bamberg
Nuremberg
Erfurt
Frankfurt
Cologne
Gastein
Salzburg
Augsburg
Schwaz
Hall
Villach
Venice
Ancona
Foligno
Subiaco
Naples
Innsbruck
Ravensburg
Mainz
Strassburg
Basel
Verona
Milan
Po
Bologna
Florence
Pisa
Tolfa
Rome
Amsterdam
Utrecht
Dordrecht
Antwerp
Malines
Leuven
St Trond
Brussels
Bruges
Bergen op Zoom
London
Bristol
Reims
Paris
Seine
Loire
Troyes
Dijon
Geneva
Lyons
Rhône
Avignon
Barcelona
Ebro
Zaragoza
Madrid
Medina del Campo
Córdoba
Seville
Cádiz
Lisbon
Tagus
Pyrenees
Kiev
Dnieper
Dniester
Carpathians
Frauenseiffen
Dvina
Vistula
Oder
Elbe
Danube
Rhine

63

31. The European Discovery of the World

1450–1600

✳ ✳ ✳

When Christopher Columbus set sail across the Atlantic in 1492, he was guided by the assertion that the circumference of the Earth was about 7000 miles shorter than

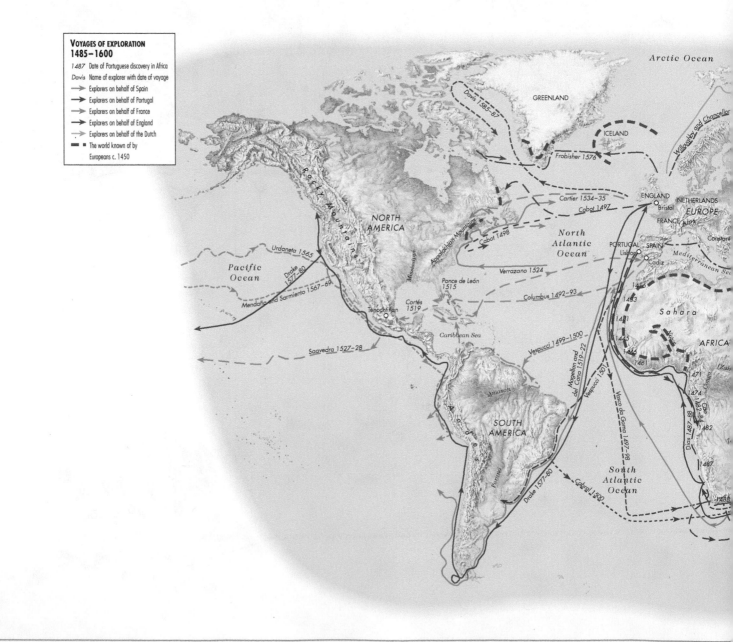

VOYAGES OF EXPLORATION
1485–1600

1487 Date of Portuguese discovery in Africa
Davis Name of explorer with date of voyage
→ Explorers on behalf of Spain
→ Explorers on behalf of Portugal
→ Explorers on behalf of France
→ Explorers on behalf of England
→ Explorers on behalf of the Dutch
- - - The world known of by Europeans c. 1450

it actually was. His belief that the West Indies were islands off the coast of China was quickly discredited when Spanish expeditions began to explore the Americas and, beyond them, the Pacific Ocean.

32. Europeans in Asia
1500–1750

* * *

The Portuguese seaborne empire was based on a series of forts linking together trading entrepots from the coast of Africa to South and Southeast Asia and on to China and Japan. This system secured Portuguese trade with the East for nearly a century. The Europeans were drawn toward Asia by the lure of exotic consumer goods—tea, spices, and silk—and by high-quality manufactured goods such as porcelain and printed cotton textiles.

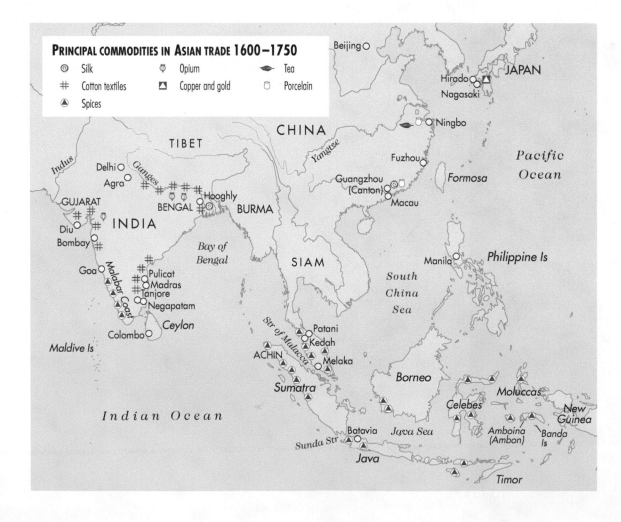

PRINCIPAL COMMODITIES IN ASIAN TRADE 1600–1750

◎ Silk　　ψ Opium　　🍃 Tea
╫ Cotton textiles　　▲ Copper and gold　　▯ Porcelain
▲ Spices

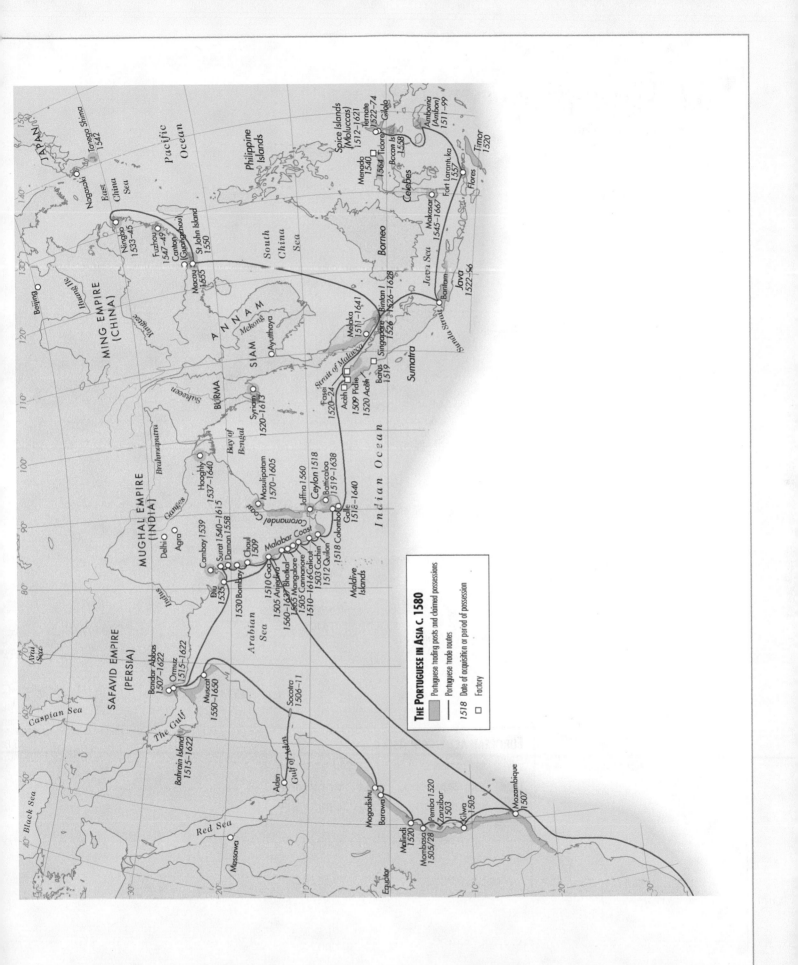

THE PORTUGUESE IN ASIA c. 1580

Portuguese trading posts and claimed possessions

Portuguese trade routes

1518 Date of acquisition or period of possession

☐ Factory

JAPAN

Tanega Shima 1542

Nagasaki

Beijing

MING EMPIRE (CHINA)

Huang He

Yangtze

Pacific Ocean

East China Sea

Ningbo 1533-45

Fuzhou 1547-49

Canton (Guangzhou)

Macau 1555

St John Island 1550

South China Sea

Philippine Islands

Spice Islands (Moluccas)

Ternate 1512-1621

Tidore 1564

Amboina (Ambon) 1511-99

Gilolo 1522-74

Becan Is 1538

Menado 1540

Celebes

Makasar 1545-1667

Fort Larantuka 1557

Flores 1520

Timor 1520

Borneo

Java Sea

Banten

Java 1522-56

ANNAM

Mekong

SIAM

Ayutthaya

BURMA

Sittreen

Brahmaputra

Syriam 1520-1613

Bay of Bengal

Bintan I 1526-1628

Melaka 1511-1641

Singapore 1526

Strait of Malacca

Sunda Strait

Sumatra

Fasei 1520-24

Aceh 1520

Pidie 1509

Barus 1519

Aceh

Indian Ocean

Hooghy 1537-1640

Masulipatam 1570-1605

Jaffna 1560

Ceylon 1518

Batticaloa 1519-1638

Galle 1518-1640

Colombo 1518

Coromandel Coast

MUGHAL EMPIRE (INDIA)

Ganges

Indus

Delhi

Agra

Camboy 1539

Surat 1540-1615

Daman 1558

Chaul 1509

Malabar Coast

Diu 1535

Bombay 1530

Goa 1510

Anjadiv 1505

Bhatkal 1560-1637

Mangalore 1565

Cannanore 1505

Calicut 1510-1616

Cochin 1503

Quilon 1512

Maldive Islands

Arabian Sea

SAFAVID EMPIRE (PERSIA)

Caspian Sea

Aral Sea

Black Sea

Bandar Abbas 1507-1622

Ormuz 1515-1622

Muscat 1550-1650

The Gulf

Bahrain Island 1515-1622

Socotra 1506-11

Gulf of Aden

Aden

Red Sea

Massowa

Equator

Mogadishu

Barawa

Malindi 1520

Mombasa 1505/28

Pemba 1520

Zanzibar 1503

Kilwa 1505

Mozambique 1507

32. Europeans in Asia

1500–1750

✳ ✳ ✳

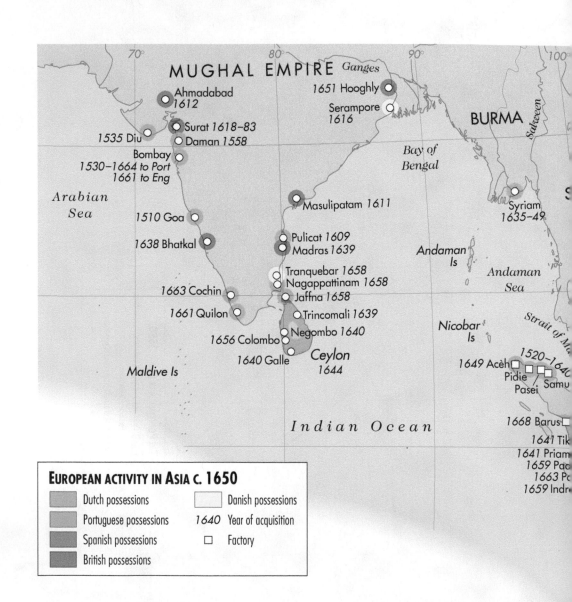

MUGHAL EMPIRE *Ganges*

1651 Hooghly

Serampore
1616

BURMA

Ahmadabad
1612

Surat 1618–83
Daman 1558

1535 Diu

Bombay
1530–1664 to Port
1661 to Eng

*Bay of
Bengal*

*Arabian
Sea*

Masulipatam 1611

Syriam
1635–49

1510 Goa

1638 Bhatkal

Pulicat 1609
Madras 1639

*Andaman
Is*

*Andaman
Sea*

Tranquebar 1658
Nagappattinam 1658

1663 Cochin

Jaffna 1658

1661 Quilon

Trincomali 1639

1656 Colombo

Negombo 1640

*Nicobar
Is*

Strait of Ma

1520–164

Maldive Is

1640 Galle

Ceylon
1644

1649 Acèh

Pidie
Pasei

Samu

Indian Ocean

1668 Barus

1641 Tik
1641 Priam
1659 Pac
1663 P
1659 Indr

European activity in Asia c. 1650

- Dutch possessions
- Portuguese possessions
- Spanish possessions
- British possessions
- Danish possessions
- 1640 Year of acquisition
- ☐ Factory

Yellow
Sea

ZIPANGU
(JAPAN)

30°

Nagasaki
1641

Tanega Shima
1542

East
China
Sea

CHINA

Ft San Salvador (Keelung)

Taiwan (Formosa)
1624–62

Pacific

Pescadores Is
1622–24

Ft Zeelandia

Ocean

20°

Yangtze

Macau
1555

Luzon

Philippine
Islands
1570

South

Mindoro

China

Panay

10°

Sea

Palawan

Negros

Mindanao
1596/1642

Sulu Arch
1638/46–63

Celebes
Sea

Morotai

Menado
1657

Djailolo

Halmahera
1653/84

Melaka 1641

Johore 1641

Sambas 1609/50

Bintan I
1628

Borneo

1657–77

Bacan I
1667

Moluccas

New
Guinea

526

mbi 1615

Sukadana 1612

Celebes
1660–77

Sula Is 1652

Bangka
1668

Buru
1622/58

Seram
1608/52

alembang
1616

Billiton
1668 Dutch Prot

Makasar
1648/67

Buton Is
1613/67

Amboina (Ambon)
1605

ra

Java Sea

Banda
Sea

Kai Is
1623/24

Aru Is
1623

da Strait

Fort Larantuka
1657

Wetar
1675

atavia (Jakarta)
1610

Java

Dili 1610/75

Tanimbar
1672

Lombok
1674

Sumbawa
1669/75

1667

1618

Timor

Kupang
1653

-10°

69

33. The Colonization of the Americas

1500–1780

✳ ✳ ✳

The Spanish crown claimed sovereignty over all American territory to the west of the line laid down at the Treaty of Tordesillas in 1494, while Portugal was given the territory to the east. Silver mining, which was concentrated in Mexico and based on the forced labor of American Indian workers, accounted for over 90 percent of Spanish-American exports between 1550 and 1640. In the Spanish Caribbean colonies of Cuba, Santo Domingo, and Puerto Rico, however, African slave labor was used to work the sugar and coffee plantations.

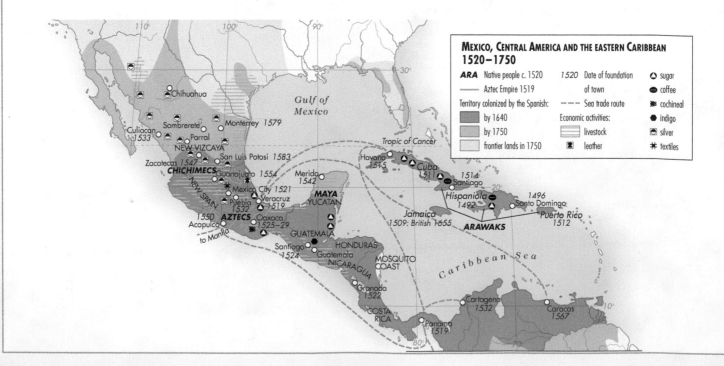

**MEXICO, CENTRAL AMERICA AND THE EASTERN CARIBBEAN
1520–1750**

ARA Native people c. 1520

— Aztec Empire 1519

Territory colonized by the Spanish:

by 1640

by 1750

frontier lands in 1750

1520 Date of foundation of town

--- Sea trade route

Economic activities:

livestock

leather

⬠ sugar

⬡ coffee

✳ cochineal

⬟ indigo

▣ silver

✳ textiles

Panama
1519

from Acapulco

Cartagena
1532

Caracas
1567

Orinoco

VENEZUELA

DUTCH
GUIANA
1667

Cayenne
1674

Bogatá 1538

COLOMBIA

Quito
1534

ECUADOR

Negro

Amazon

Equator

Maranhão
1612

Tumbes
1526

Xingu

Madeira

B R A Z I L

line of Treaty of Tordesillas 1494

Recife
1535, Pernambuco

PERU

Lima
1535

Cuzco
1534

São Francisco

GOIÁS

MATO GROSSO

MINAS
GERAIS

Bahia
1549

Potosí
1545

Paraguay

Paraná

40°

20°

Tropic of Capricorn

Rio De Janeiro
1565

Asunción
1537

Valparaíso
1544

Santiago
1542

Buenos Aires
1536,
refounded 1580

Montevideo
1726

30°

50°

60°

Valdivia
1552

PATAGONIA

40°

60°

50°

70°

SPANISH AND PORTUGUESE SOUTH AMERICA 1525–1750

▨ Inca Empire 1525	▨ Dutch colony	◈ mining
Spanish settlement:	▨ French colony	◈ cocoa
▨ to 1640	▨ Jesuit mission state	▢ mercury
▨ to 1750	**Economic activities:**	▨ hides
▨ frontier lands 1750	◐ coffee	▼ wine
Portuguese settlement:	△ sugar	- - - Sea trade route
▨ to 1640	△ mixed agriculture	—— Land trade route
▨ to 1750	▨ silver	
▨ frontier lands 1750	◉ gold	

33. The Colonization of the Americas

1500–1780

* * *

The Spanish Empire in North America was vast, but it attracted few settlers, and there was virtually no economic development outside Florida. The French Empire, although large, was thinly populated, and its limited economic development was based on fishing and the fur trade. By contrast, the British Empire had the least extensive territory, but it developed a rich, diverse, and populous economy and an extensive overseas trade.

COLONIZATION OF THE NORTH AMERICAN MAINLAND TO 1750

HUR Native American people

British settlement:
to 1640
to 1750
frontier lands in 1750

Spanish settlement:
to 1750
frontier lands in 1750

French settlement:
to 1750
frontier lands in 1750

Economic activity c. 1750:
mixed agriculture
fishing
trapping
cattle
grain
tobacco
rice
indigo
timber
shipbuilding
ironworks
trade route

Santa Fe

El Paso

Rio Grande

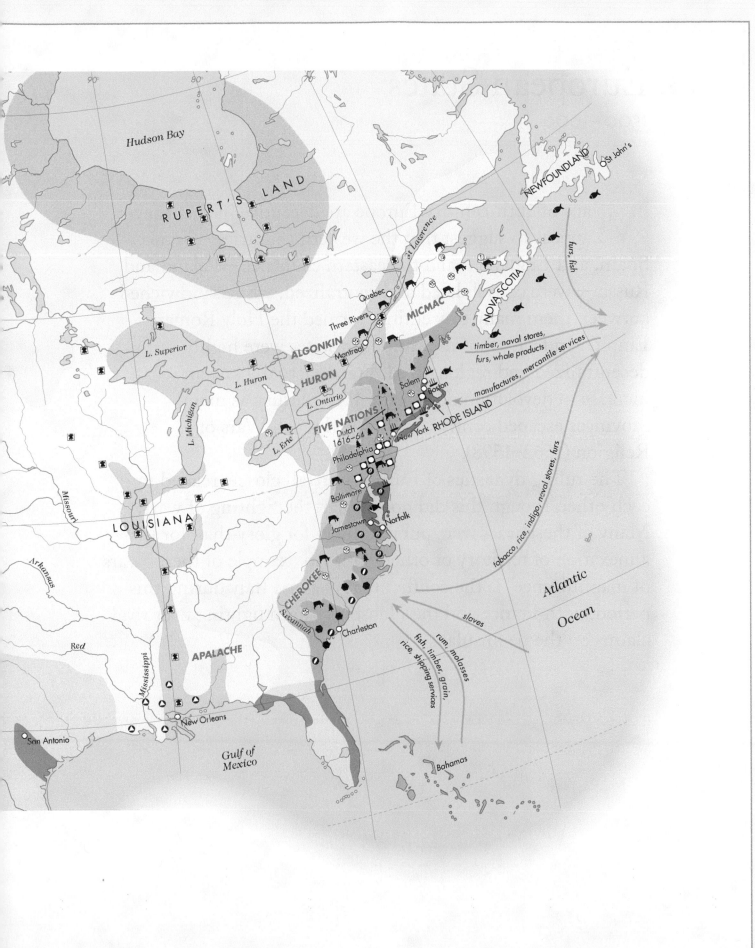

Hudson Bay

RUPERT'S LAND

NEWFOUNDLAND

St John's

NOVA SCOTIA

St Lawrence

Quebec

MICMAC

Three Rivers

ALGONKIN

Montreal

HURON

L. Superior

L. Huron

L. Michigan

L. Ontario

L. Erie

Salem

Boston

FIVE NATIONS

Dutch
1616-64

New York

RHODE ISLAND

Philadelphia

Baltimore

Jamestown

Norfolk

LOUISIANA

Missouri

Arkansas

CHEROKEE

Red

Savannah

Charleston

APALACHE

Mississippi

New Orleans

San Antonio

Gulf of
Mexico

Bahamas

Atlantic

Ocean

furs, fish

timber, naval stores,
furs, whale products

manufactures, mercantile services

tobacco, rice, indigo, naval stores, furs

slaves

fish, timber, grain,
rice, shipping services

rum, molasses

34. European States

1500–1600

* * *

Maps of 16th-century Europe are deceptive in that they appear to suggest that the western countries—France, Spain, and England—and the eastern countries—Poland and Russia—were consolidated and centralized, while sandwiched between them many tiny entities formed the Holy Roman Empire. In fact, all of the European states were highly decentralized and regionalized. France actually saw an increase in devolution during the 16th century as many provinces escaped control during the French Wars of Religion (1562–1598).

The ruling dynasties of Europe were all closely related to each other, though this did not prevent the fighting of wars. Many of these wars were pursued more for glory than for the annexation of territory or other gain. An example of these "wars of magnificence" is the conflict that plagued Italy during this period, with France and the Habsburgs both fighting over rival claims on the peninsula.

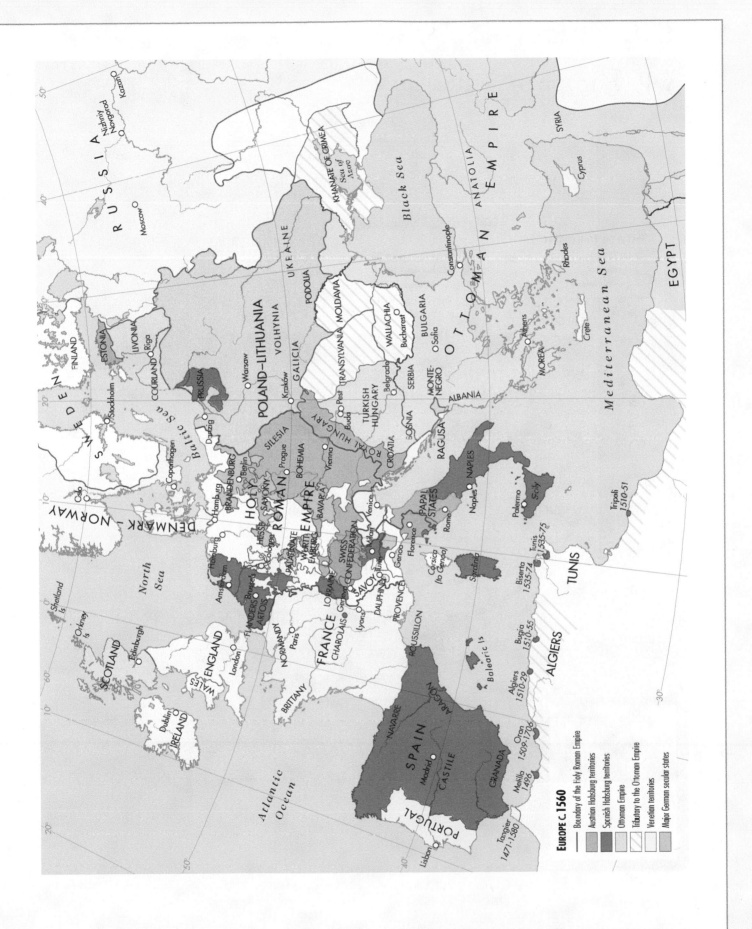

EUROPE c. 1560

Boundary of the Holy Roman Empire
Austrian Habsburg territories
Spanish Habsburg territories
Ottoman Empire
Tributary to the Ottoman Empire
Venetian territories
Major German secular states

RUSSIA

Nizhniy Novgorod ○
Kazan ○

Moscow ○

SWEDEN

FINLAND

ESTONIA
LIVONIA
Riga ○
CCURLAND

Stockholm ○

Baltic Sea

Copenhagen ○
Danzig ○

PRUSSIA

Warsaw ○

POLAND–LITHUANIA

VOLHYNIA
GALICIA
PODOLIA

UKRAINE

KHANATE OF CRIMEA
Sea of Azov

Black Sea

SYRIA

ANATOLIA

OTTOMAN EMPIRE

Constantinople ○

Cyprus

Rhodes

EGYPT

Mediterranean Sea

Crete

MOREA

Athens ○

ALBANIA

MONTE-NEGRO

SERBIA
BOSNIA
RAGUSA

BULGARIA
Sofia ○
Belgrade ○

WALLACHIA
Bucharest ○

MOLDAVIA
TRANSYLVANIA

TURKISH HUNGARY
Pest ○
Buda ○
ROYAL HUNGARY
CROATIA

Kraków ○

SILESIA
BOHEMIA
Prague ○

Vienna ○

BRANDENBURG
Berlin ○

SAXONY

HOLY ROMAN EMPIRE

BAVARIA

Venice ○

PAPAL STATES
Rome ○

NAPLES
Naples ○
Palermo ○
Sicily

Tripoli
1510-51

TUNIS

Biserta 1535-74
Tunis 1535-75

Sardinia

Bugia 1510-55

ALGIERS

Algiers 1510-29

Oran 1509-1706

Melilla 1496

Balearic Is

Corsica (to Genoa)

Florence ○
Genoa ○

Milan ○

SWISS CONFEDERATION
Geneva ○

SAVOY

DAUPHINÉ

PROVENCE

ROUSSILLON

LORRAINE

WÜRT EMBURG

PALATINATE
Cologne ○

HESSE

Hamburg ○

Amsterdam ○
Brussels ○
FLANDERS
ARTOIS

DENMARK–NORWAY

NORWAY

Oslo ○

North Sea

Shetland Is

Orkney Is

SCOTLAND
Edinburgh ○

ENGLAND
London ○

WALES

IRELAND
Dublin ○

Atlantic Ocean

BRITTANY

NORMANDY
Paris ○

FRANCE
CHAROLAIS

Lyons ○

SPAIN
Madrid ○
CASTILE

NAVARRE
ARAGON

GRANADA

PORTUGAL
Lisbon ○

Tangier 1471-1580

75

34. European States

1500–1600

✳ ✳ ✳

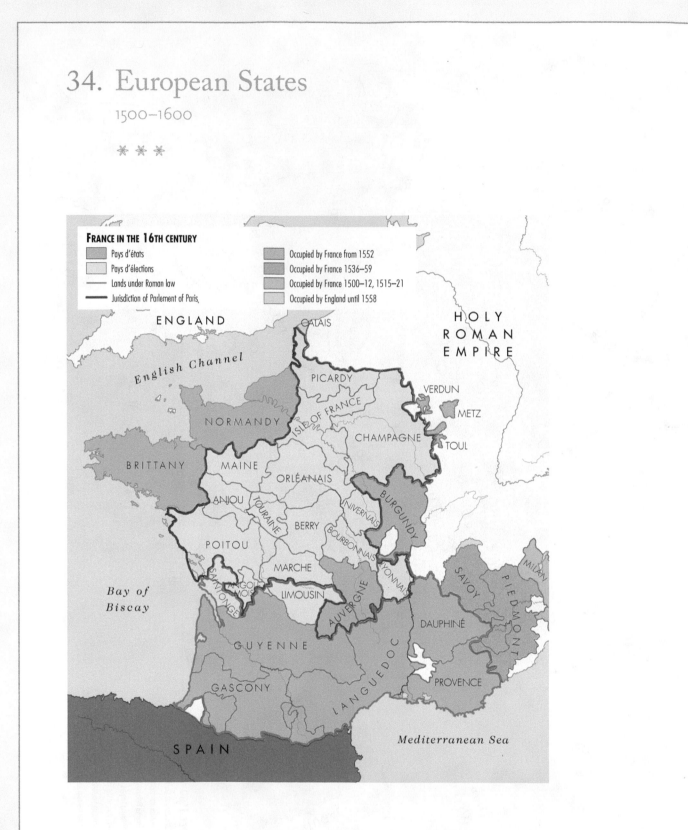

FRANCE IN THE 16TH CENTURY

- Pays d'états
- Pays d'élections
- Lands under Roman law
- Jurisdiction of Parlement of Paris
- Occupied by France from 1552
- Occupied by France 1536–59
- Occupied by France 1500–12, 1515–21
- Occupied by England until 1558

ENGLAND

English Channel

HOLY ROMAN EMPIRE

CALAIS

PICARDY

ISLE OF FRANCE

NORMANDY

VERDUN

METZ

CHAMPAGNE

TOUL

BRITTANY

MAINE

ORLÉANAIS

ANJOU

TOURAINE

NIVERNAIS

BURGUNDY

BERRY

BOURBONNAIS

POITOU

LYONNAIS

MARCHE

SAINTONGE

ANGOUMOIS

LIMOUSIN

AUVERGNE

SAVOY

MILAN

PIEDMONT

DAUPHINÉ

Bay of Biscay

GUYENNE

LANGUEDOC

GASCONY

PROVENCE

Mediterranean Sea

SPAIN

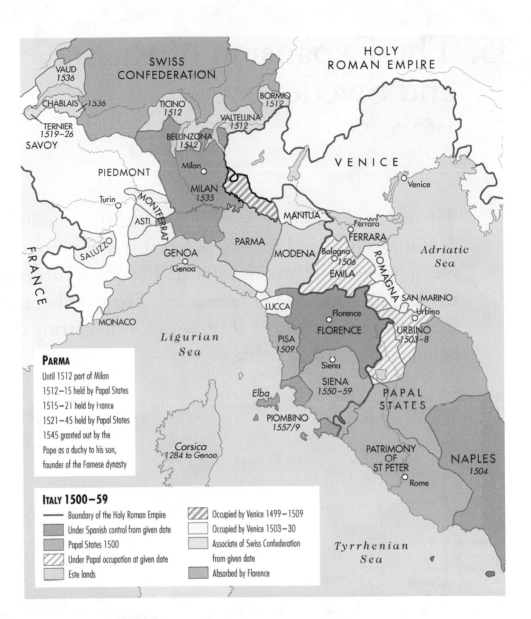

HOLY ROMAN EMPIRE

SWISS CONFEDERATION

VAUD
1536

CHABLAIS 1536

TERNIER
1519–26

SAVOY

TICINO
1512

BORMIO
1512

VALTELLINA
1512

BELLINZONA
1512

PIEDMONT

Milan

MILAN
1535

Turin

MONFERRAT

ASTI

SALUZZO

FRANCE

GENOA

Genoa

MONACO

MANTUA

VENICE

Ferrara

FERRARA

Venice

Adriatic
Sea

PARMA

MODENA

Bologna
1506

EMILA

ROMAGNA

SAN MARINO

Ligurian
Sea

LUCCA

PISA
1509

Florence

FLORENCE

Siena

SIENA
1550–59

Urbino

URBINO
1503–8

Elba

PIOMBINO
1557/9

Corsica
1284 to Genoa

PAPAL
STATES

PATRIMONY
OF
ST PETER

Rome

NAPLES
1504

Tyrrhenian
Sea

PARMA

Until 1512 part of Milan

1512–15 held by Papal States

1515–21 held by France

1521–45 held by Papal States

1545 granted out by the
Pope as a duchy to his son,
founder of the Farnese dynasty

ITALY 1500–59

— Boundary of the Holy Roman Empire

  Under Spanish control from given date

  Papal States 1500

  Under Papal occupation at given date

  Este lands

  Occupied by Venice 1499–1509

  Occupied by Venice 1503–30

  Associate of Swiss Confederation
  from given date

  Absorbed by Florence

35. The Expansion of Russia and Sweden

1462–1795

✳ ✳ ✳

Russian expansion eastward involved the establishment of *ostrogs* (fortified trading posts) at strategic points. An *ostrog* was founded at Tomsk in 1604, and by 1607 Turuchansk on the Yenisei River had been reached. The river became the frontier of the empire in 1619, with another string of *ostrogs* being established along it.

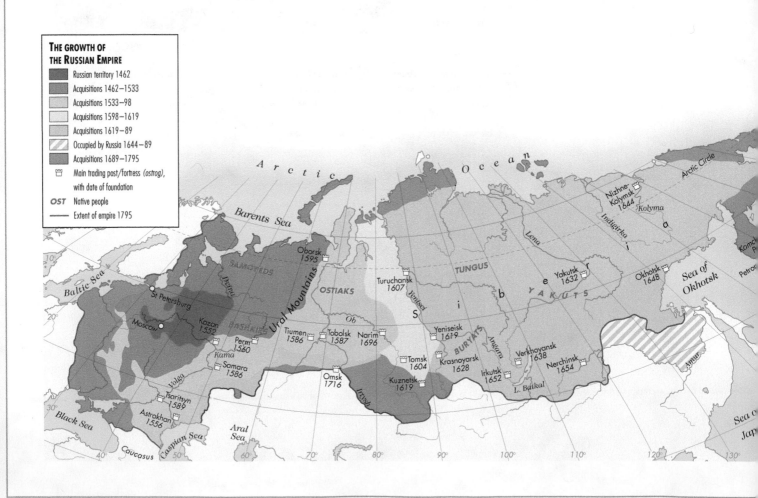

THE GROWTH OF THE RUSSIAN EMPIRE

- Russian territory 1462
- Acquisitions 1462–1533
- Acquisitions 1533–98
- Acquisitions 1598–1619
- Acquisitions 1619–89
- Occupied by Russia 1644–89
- Acquisitions 1689–1795
- ⊡ Main trading post/fortress (*ostrog*), with date of foundation
- **OST** Native people
- — Extent of empire 1795

LAPLAND

Arctic Circle

Arkhangelsk

S W E D E N

tallow, leather, potash, grain

TRONDHEIM

JÄMTLAND

HÄRJEDALEN

DENMARK – NORWAY

1389

BOHUSLÄN

HALLAND

Älvsborg

The Sound

BLEKINGE

SKÅNE

1592–1604

Stralsund

Lübeck

Hamburg

Wismar

POMERANIA

Stettin

BREMEN-VERDEN

BRANDENBURG

Stockholm

timber, copper, iron

to London
and
Amsterdam

Danzig

PRUSSIA

Elbing

grain

grain

POLAND

1569

FINLAND

CARELIA

INGRIA

Reval

ESTONIA

Dorpat

LIVONIA

flax, hemp, hides

grain

flax, hemp
timber, grain

Riga

COURLAND

flax, hemp
timber, grain

Königsberg

LITHUANIA

Novgorod

RUSSIA

In the 16th century Sweden was a small country of just over
a million people. However, with the aid of its natural resources,
it built a Baltic empire, reaching the summit of its power
between 1621 and 1660.

36. The Reformation and Counter-Reformation

* * *

Protestantism took a number of forms across Europe. In Germany and Scandinavia local secular rulers promoted the establishment of new churches, mostly along Lutheran lines. In the Netherlands, Calvinism became politically predominant during the later 16th century, while in England the Anglican Church was established by Henry VIII. Further east, Calvinism was adopted in Transylvania (in Hungary), and in Poland so many nobles became Protestant that special provisions for their toleration had to be agreed in 1569–1571. Switzerland was a major powerhouse of the Protestant Reformation but was intensely divided. French Protestantism was overwhelmingly urban. Crucial to its survival, however, was the support of a very large minority of the nobility.

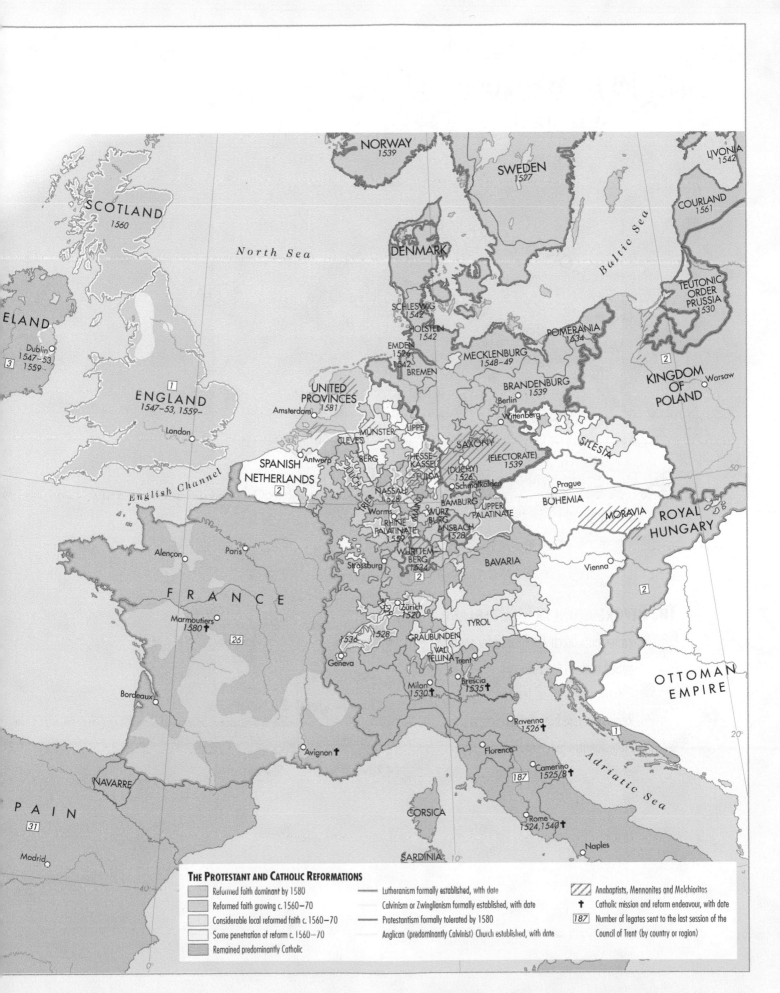

THE PROTESTANT AND CATHOLIC REFORMATIONS

NORWAY
1539

SWEDEN
1527

LIVONIA
1542

COURLAND
1561

SCOTLAND
1560

North Sea

DENMARK

Baltic Sea

TEUTONIC
ORDER
PRUSSIA
1530

ELAND

Dublin
1547–53,
1559

3

SCHLESWIG
1542

HOLSTEIN
1542

POMERANIA
1634

ENGLAND
1547–53, 1559–

1

UNITED
PROVINCES
1581

Amsterdam

EMDEN
1526
1542
BREMEN

MECKLENBURG
1548–49

BRANDENBURG
1539

Berlin

2

KINGDOM
OF
POLAND

Warsaw

London

MÜNSTER
LIPPE

CLEVES

Antwerp

SPANISH
NETHERLANDS

2

BERG

SAXONY

(ELECTORATE)
1539

Wittenberg

SILESIA

HESSE-
KASSEL
FULDA

(DUCHY)
1526

Schmalkalden

Prague

BOHEMIA

MORAVIA

ROYAL
HUNGARY

English Channel

JÜLICH

NASSAU
1528

TRIER

RHINE
PALATINATE
1559

Worms

BAMBERG

WÜRZ-
BURG

ANSBACH
1528

UPPER
PALATINATE

Alençon

Paris

Vienna

2

F R A N C E

WÜRTTEM-
BERG
1534

2

BAVARIA

Strassburg

Marmoutiers
1580 †

26

Zürich
1520

TYROL

1536

1528

GRAUBUNDEN

VAL
TELLINA

Trent

Geneva

Milan
1530 †

Brescia
1635 †

OTTOMAN
EMPIRE

Bordeaux

Ravenna
1526 †

Adriatic Sea

Avignon †

Florence

Camerino
1525/8

NAVARRE

CORSICA

187

Rome
1524, 1540 †

PAIN

31

SARDINIA

Naples

Madrid

THE PROTESTANT AND CATHOLIC REFORMATIONS

Reformed faith dominant by 1580	—— Lutheranism formally established, with date
Reformed faith growing c. 1560–70	Calvinism or Zwinglianism formally established, with date
Considerable local reformed faith c. 1560–70	—— Protestantism formally tolerated by 1580
Some penetration of reform c. 1560–70	Anglican (predominantly Calvinist) Church established, with date
Remained predominantly Catholic	

Anabaptists, Mennonites and Melchiorites

† Catholic mission and reform endeavour, with date

187 Number of legates sent to the last session of the Council of Trent (by country or region)

36. The Reformation and Counter-Reformation

* * *

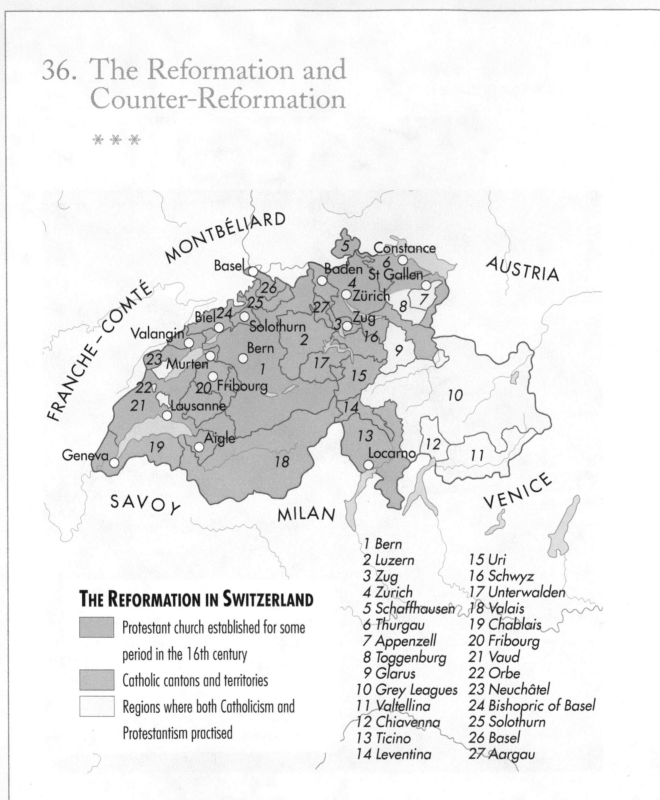

MONTBÉLIARD

FRANCHE-COMTÉ

AUSTRIA

Basel

5
Constance
Baden
6
St Gallen
4
Zürich
8
7
26
25
27
24
Biel
3
Zug
Valangin
Solothurn
2
16
Bern
9
23
Murten
1
17
15
22
20
Fribourg
21
Lausanne
14
10
Aigle
13
12
19
Locarno
11
Geneva
18

SAVOY

MILAN

VENICE

THE REFORMATION IN SWITZERLAND

Protestant church established for some period in the 16th century

Catholic cantons and territories

Regions where both Catholicism and Protestantism practised

1 Bern	
2 Luzern	15 Uri
3 Zug	16 Schwyz
4 Zürich	17 Unterwalden
5 Schaffhausen	18 Valais
6 Thurgau	19 Chablais
7 Appenzell	20 Fribourg
8 Toggenburg	21 Vaud
9 Glarus	22 Orbe
10 Grey Leagues	23 Neuchâtel
11 Valtellina	24 Bishopric of Basel
12 Chiavenna	25 Solothurn
13 Ticino	26 Basel
14 Leventina	27 Aargau

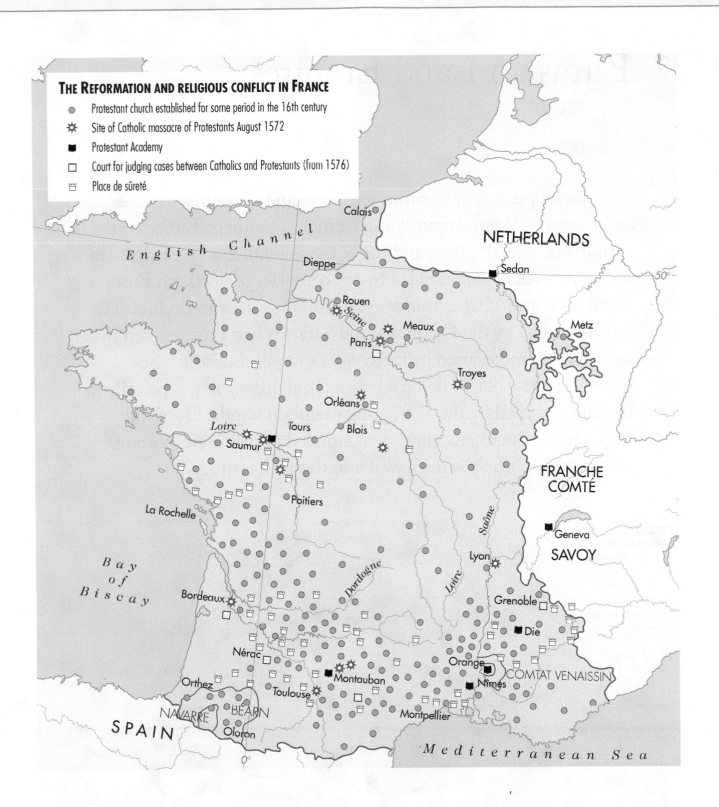

THE REFORMATION AND RELIGIOUS CONFLICT IN FRANCE

● Protestant church established for some period in the 16th century

✸ Site of Catholic massacre of Protestants August 1572

■ Protestant Academy

☐ Court for judging cases between Catholics and Protestants (from 1576)

⛉ Place de sûreté

Calais

NETHERLANDS

English Channel

Dieppe

Sedan

50°

Metz

Rouen

Seine

Meaux

Paris

Troyes

Orléans

FRANCHE
COMTÉ

Loire

Tours

Blois

Saumur

Poitiers

La Rochelle

Saône

Geneva

SAVOY

*Bay
of
Biscay*

Lyon

Dordogne

Bordeaux

Grenoble

Loire

Die

Nérac

Orange

Montauban

COMTAT VENAISSIN

Orthez

Nîmes

Toulouse

Montpellier

NAVARRE

BÉARN

SPAIN

Oloron

Mediterranean Sea

37. Eurasian Land Empires
ca. 1700

* * *

Despite periods of vigorous territorial and economic expansion, the great land empires of western and southern Eurasia—the Ottomans, the Mughals, and the Safavids—failed to participate in the commercial revolution led by the countries of northern Europe in the 17th and 18th centuries—by 1700 they were in decline. The territory ruled by the Ottomans and Safavids was criss-crossed by land and sea routes used by merchants and pilgrims alike. Sea travel was risky but could be relatively straightforward, especially in regions governed by the alternating monsoon winds. Overland traffic was arduous and slow but continued to play an important role in trade with Asia until well into the 18th century.

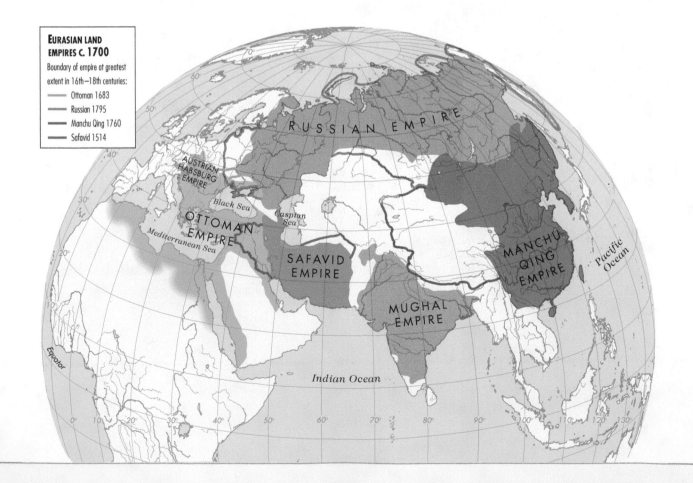

EURASIAN LAND EMPIRES C. 1700

Boundary of empire at greatest extent in 16th–18th centuries:

——— Ottoman 1683
——— Russian 1795
——— Manchu Qing 1760
——— Safavid 1514

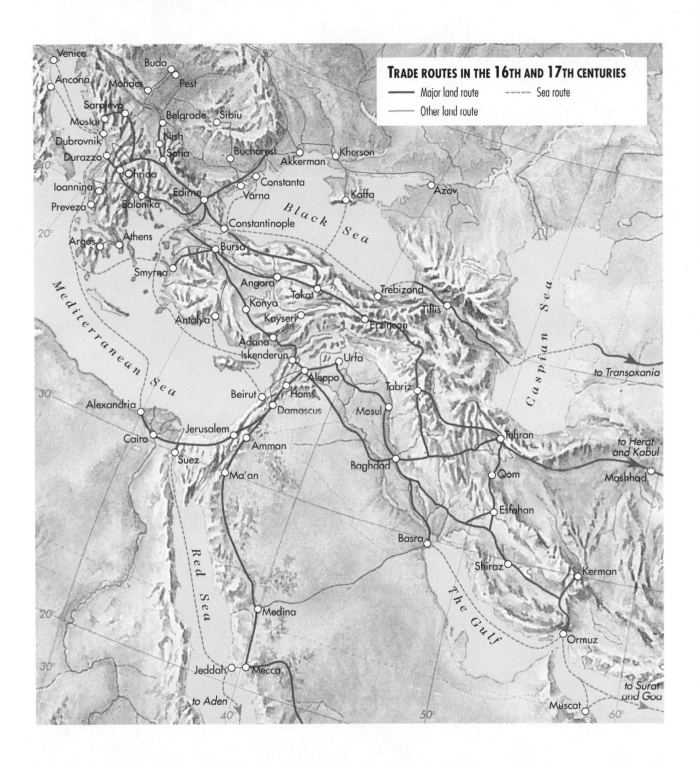

TRADE ROUTES IN THE 16TH AND 17TH CENTURIES

——— Major land route ----- Sea route
——— Other land route

Venice
Ancona
Buda
Pest
Mohacs
Sarajevo
Mostar
Belgrade
Sibiu
Nish
Dubrovnik
Sofia
Bucharest
Durazzo
Ohrida
Akkerman
Kherson
Constanta
Edirne
Varna
Kaffa
Azov
Ioannina
Preveza
Salonika
Athens
Constantinople
Argos
Bursa
Black Sea
Smyrna
Angora
Tokat
Trebizond
Konya
Kayseri
Tiflis
Antalya
Erzincan
Adana
Iskenderun
Urfa
Mediterranean Sea
Aleppo
Tabriz
Beirut
Homs
Mosul
Caspian Sea
Damascus
Alexandria
Jerusalem
Tehran
Cairo
Amman
Baghdad
to Transoxania
Suez
Qom
to Herat and Kabul
Ma'an
Esfahan
Mashhad
Basra
Shiraz
Kerman
The Gulf
Red Sea
Medina
Ormuz
Jeddah
Mecca
to Surat and Goa
to Aden
Muscat

20°
30°
40°
50°
60°
40°

Outline Maps

Sumer and the Ancient Near East

* * *

1. Identify and label the following regions:
   a) Fertile Crescent
   b) Sumer
   c) Akkadia
   d) Egypt
   e) Anatolia
   f) Mespotamia

2. Identify and label the following rivers and bodies of water:
   a) Tigris
   b) Euphrates
   c) Mediterranean Sea
   d) Persian Gulf
   e) Red Sea
   f) Nile River

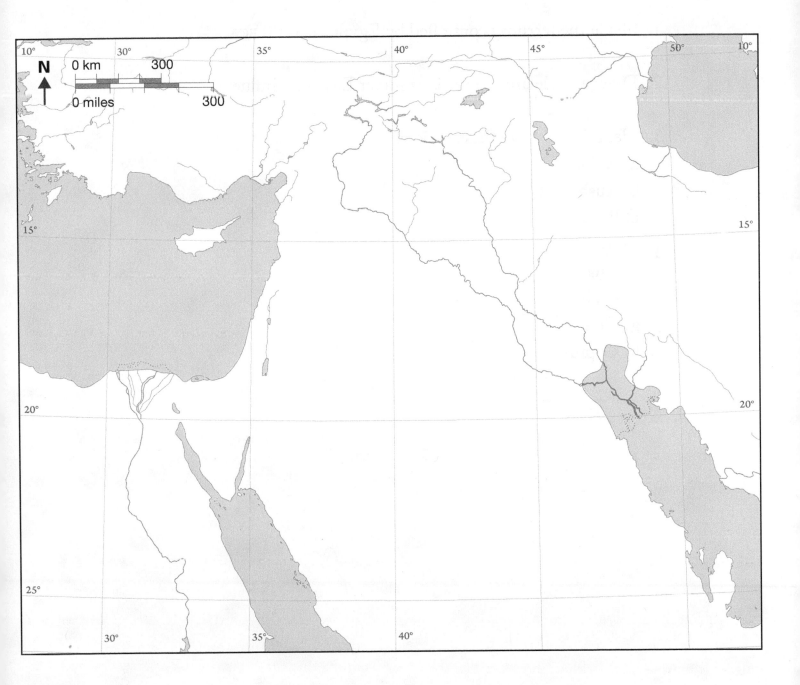

Middle and New Kingdom Egypt

* * *

1. Shade the territory controlled by Egypt ca. 1500 BCE.

2. Draw a circle around the area under Egyptian influence.

3. Identify and label these regions:
   a) Nubia
   b) Kush
   c) Punt
   d) Syria
   e) Sinai
   f) Arabia
   g) Crete
   h) Cyprus

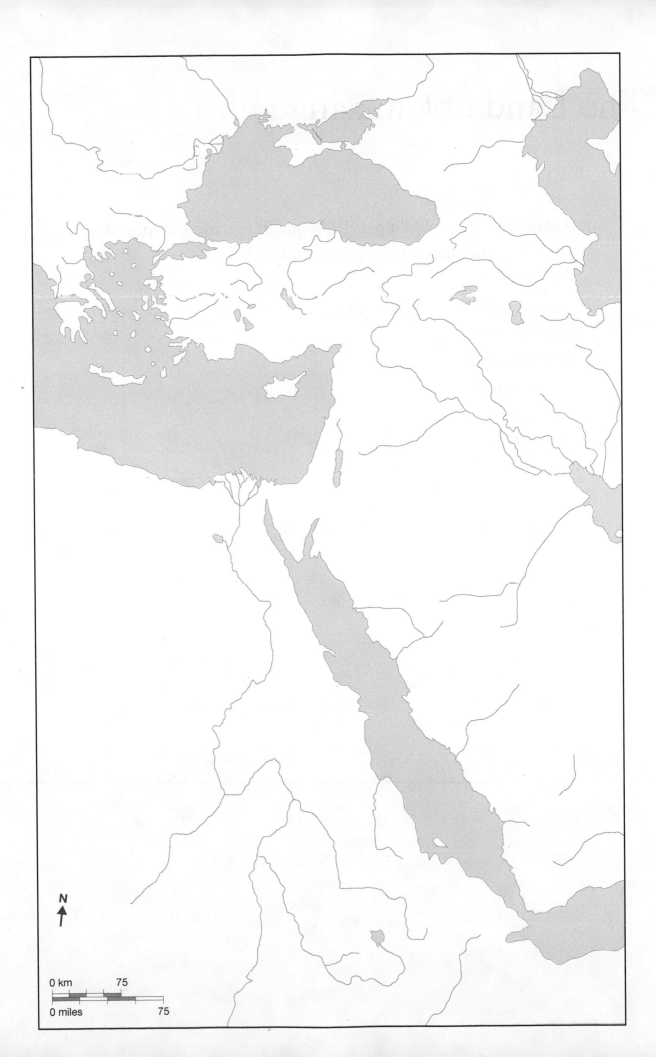

The Land of Canaan

* * *

1. Using different colored pencils, shade in the area comprised by Judah and the area comprised by Israel.

2. Identify and label these regions:
   a) Jerusalem
   b) Phoenecia
   c) Damascus
   d) Sea of Galilee
   e) Dead Sea

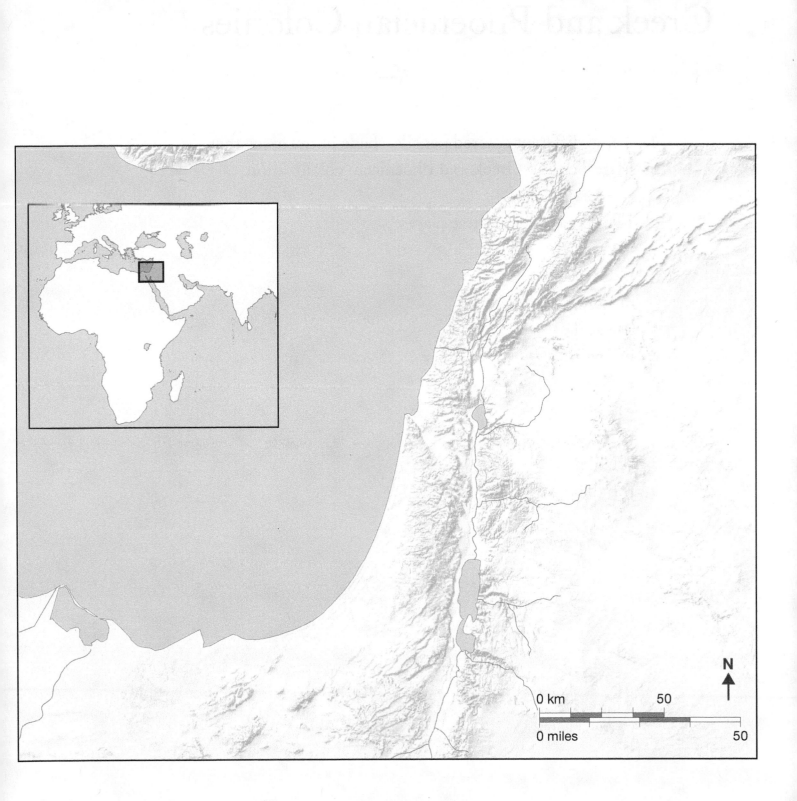

0 km   50

0 miles   50

N

Greek and Phoenician Colonies

* * *

1. Using different colored pencils, shade in the areas that correspond to Greek and Phoenician colonization.

2. Identify and label these places:
   a) Asia Minor
   b) Greece
   c) Italy
   d) Gaul
   e) Spain
   f) Sicily
   g) Carthage
   h) Athens
   i) Miletus
   j) Byblos

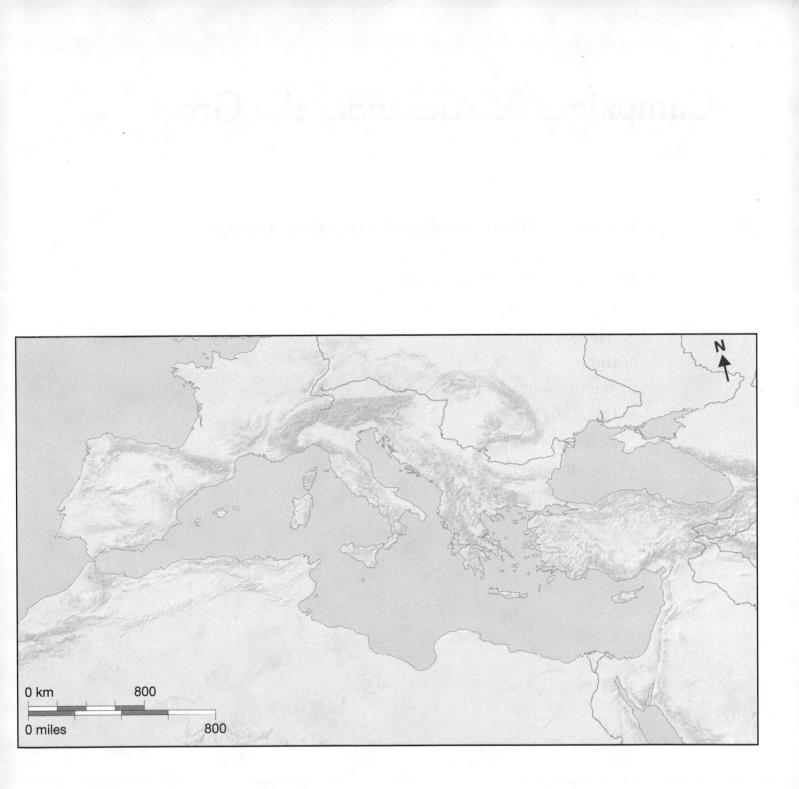

0 km   800

0 miles   800

Campaigns of Alexander the Great

*** *** ***

1. Use a pencil to draw the route of Alexander's campaigns.

2. Identify and label these places:
   a) Persia
   b) Macedonia
   c) India
   d) Bactria
   e) Indus River
   f) Persepolis
   g) Alexandria (Egypt)

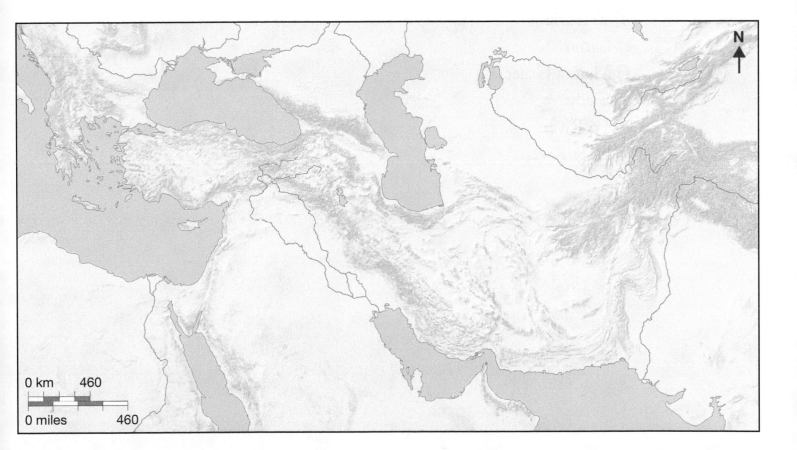

Archaic Italy

*** * ***

1. Identify and label these places:
   a) Alps
   b) Apennines
   c) Rome
   d) Ertruria
   e) Latium
   f) Magna Graecia
   g) Sicily
   h) Po River
   i) Tiber River

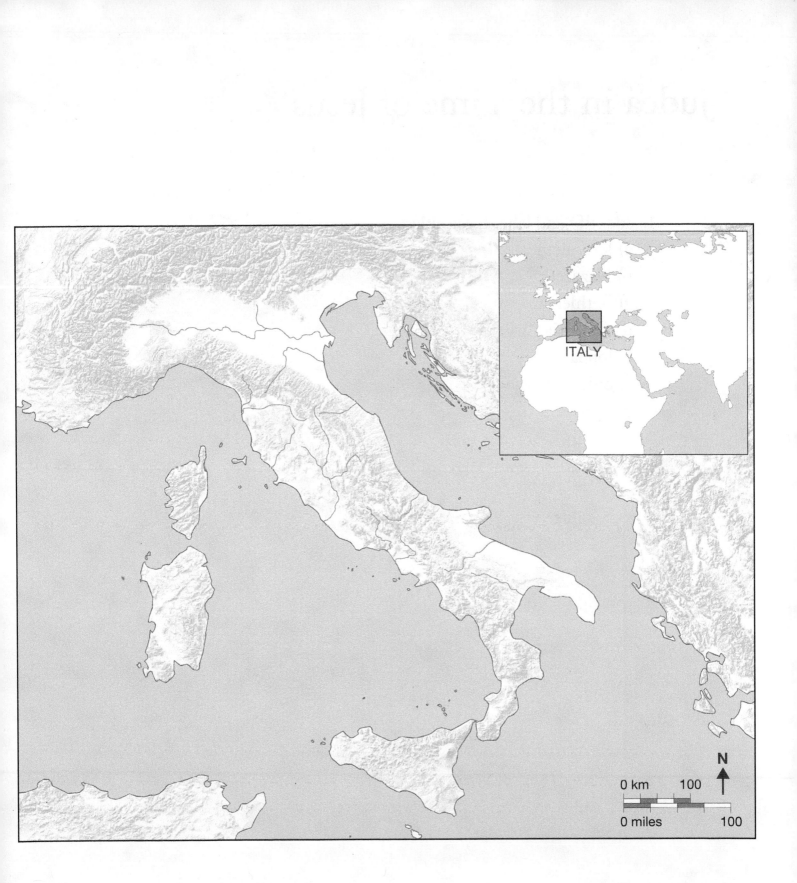

ITALY

0 km 100

0 miles 100

N

99

Judea in the Time of Jesus

* * *

1. Identify and label these cities:
   a) Jerusalem
   b) Nazareth
   c) Bethlehem
   d) Caesaria
   e) Joppa
   f) Sidon
   g) Tyre

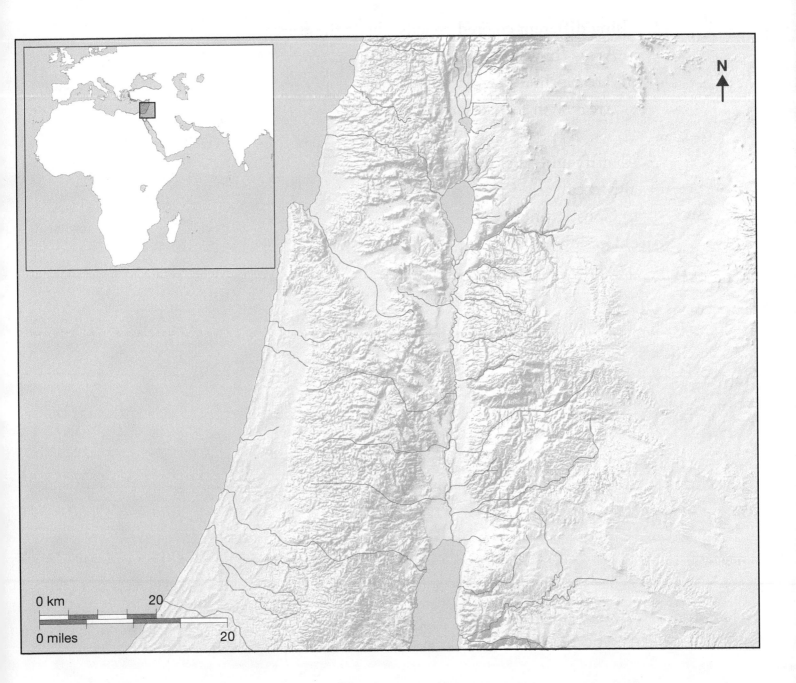

Arabia in the 6th Century CE

* * *

1. Using different colored pencils, shade these areas:
   a) Areas converted to Christianity
   b) Areas primarily Zorastrian
   c) Areas with Jewish settlements

2. Identify and label these places:
   a) Mecca
   b) Constantinople
   c) Ctesiphon
   d) Medina (Yathrib)

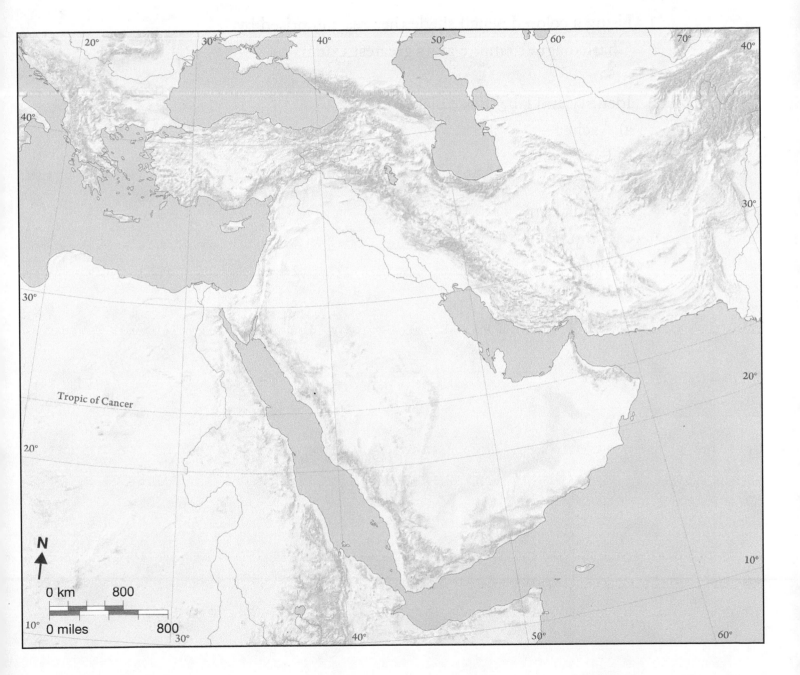

Tropic of Cancer

N

0 km   800

0 miles   800

Charlemagne's Empire

* * *

1. Using a colored pencil shade the area comprised by Charlemagne's empire at its greatest extent.

2. Identify and label these places:
   a) Aachen
   b) Paris
   c) Saxony
   d) Lindisfarne
   e) Burgundy
   f) Normandy
   g) Brittany
   h) Monte Cassino

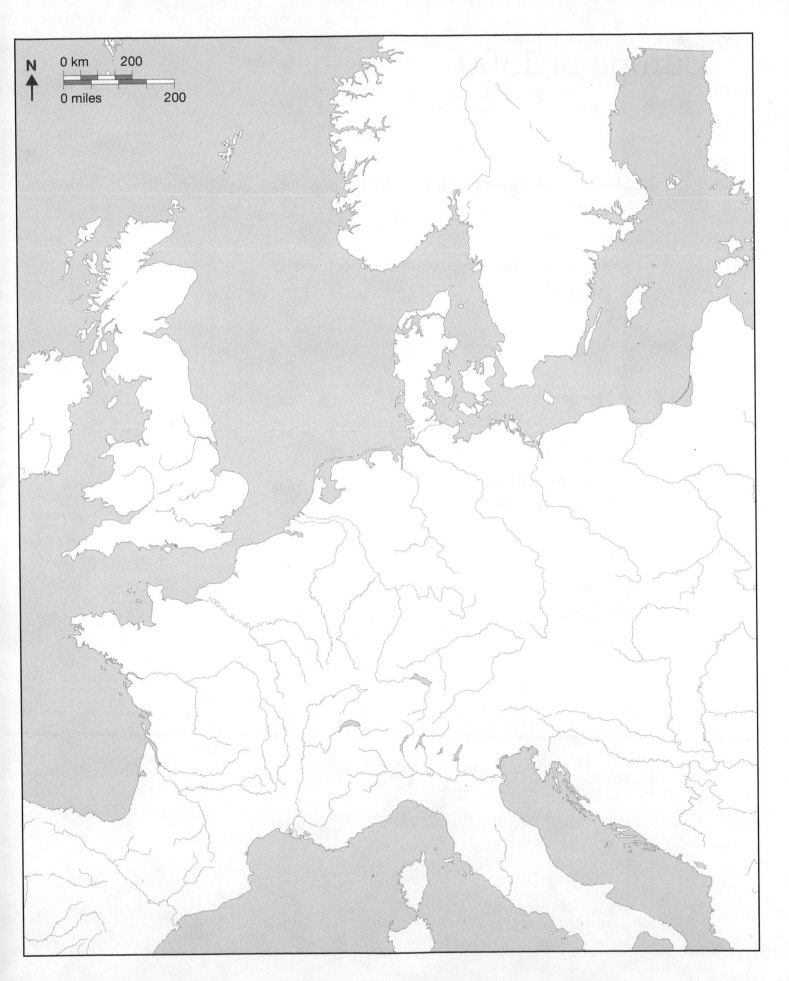

Europe in 1300

* * *

1. Shade those regions with the highest population density in 1300.

2. Identify and label these regions and countries:
   a) Portugal
   b) Castile
   c) Aragon
   d) France
   e) Flanders
   f) Ireland
   g) England
   h) Holy Roman Empire
   i) Norway and Sweden
   j) Poland
   k) Lithuania
   l) Serbia
   m) Hungary
   n) Russia

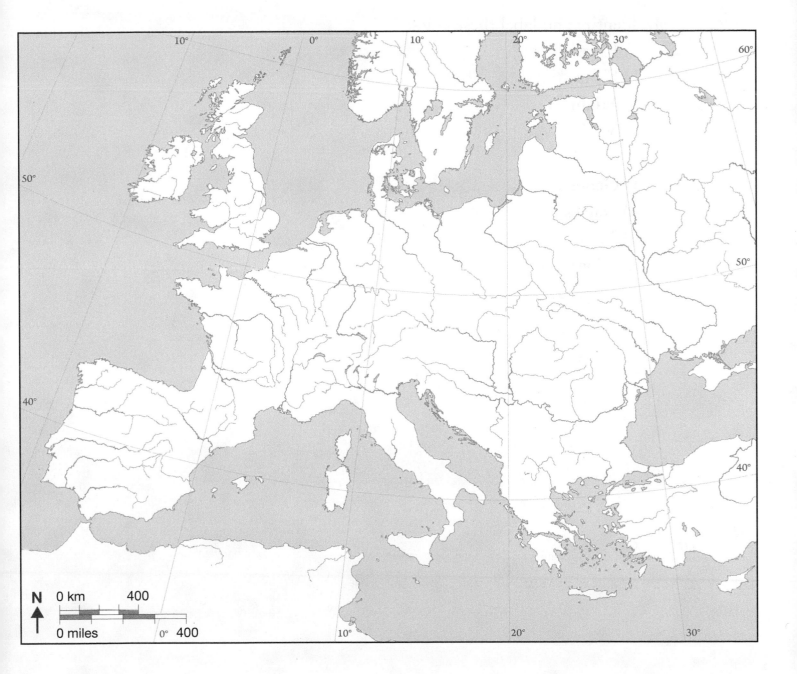

Renaissance Italy

* * *

1. Identify and label these cities:
   a) Florence
   b) Siena
   c) Milan
   d) Venice
   e) Rome
   f) Genoa
   g) Naples
   h) Mantua
   i) Bologna
   j) Palermo

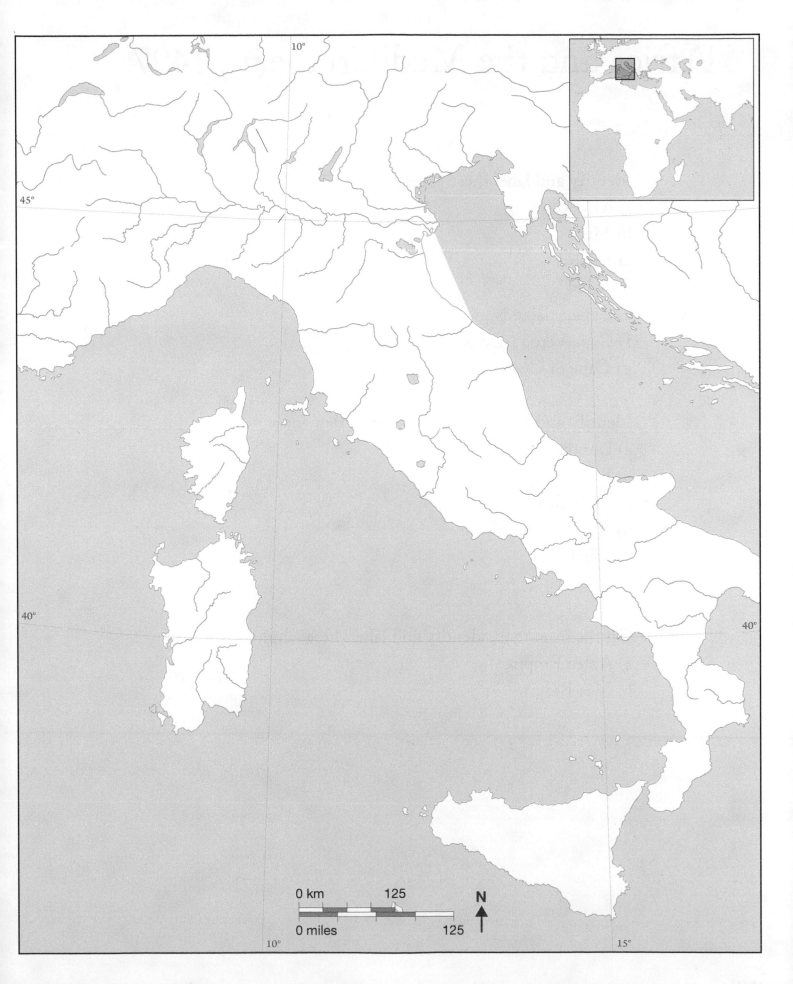

10°

45°

40°   40°

0 km   125

0 miles   125   N

10°   15°

Africa and the Mediterranean, 1497

* * *

1. Identify and label these places:
   a) Morocco
   b) Mali
   c) Sahara
   d) Sahel
   e) Canary Islands
   f) Cape Verde Islands
   g) Cape of Good Hope

2. Identify and label these cities and settlements:
   a) Lisbon
   b) Seville
   c) Timbuktu
   d) São Jorge da Mina
   e) Mina
   f) Calicut

3. On the inset map, identify and label these empires:
   a) Aztec Empire
   b) Inca Empire

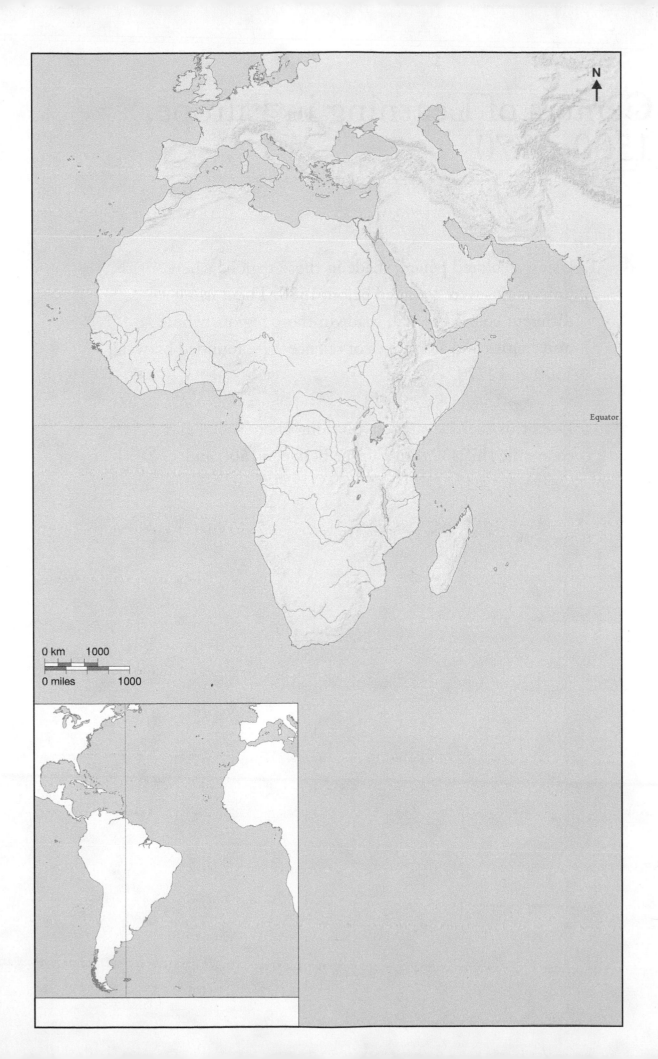

N

Equator

0 km   1000
0 miles   1000

Centers of Learning in Europe, 1500–1770

* * *

1. Using a colored pencil, shade in those regions where universities were founded before 1500. Then, using a different colored pencil, shade in those regions where universities and academies of science were founded between 1500 and 1770.

   Does this exercise suggest anything about social and economic shifts within Europe between 1500 and 1770?

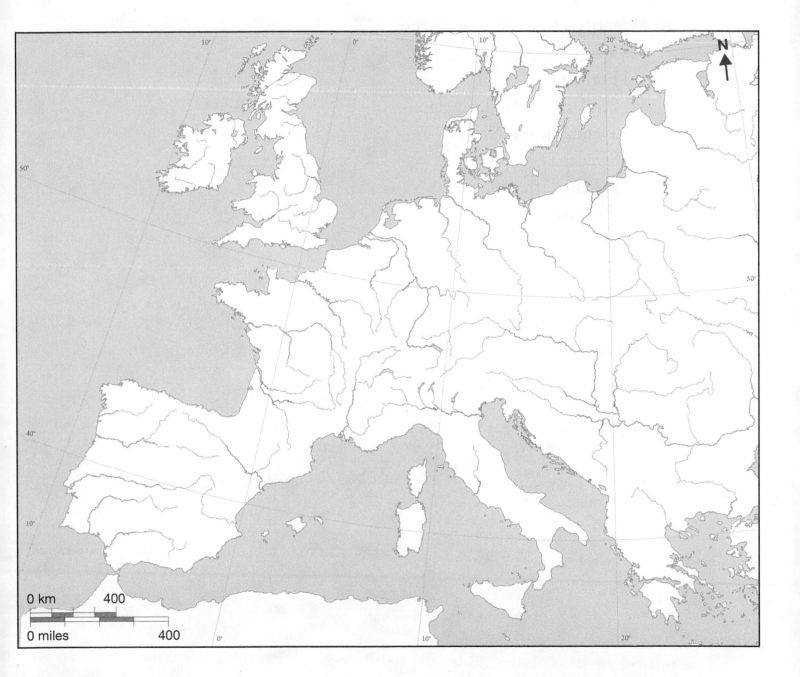

Europe in 1648

* * *

1. Identify and label these places:
   a) Spain
   b) Portugal
   c) Scotland, Ireland, England
   d) Denmark and Norway
   e) Sweden
   f) Poland-Lithuania
   g) Ottoman Empire
   h) Austria
   i) Hungary
   j) Papal States
   k) Switzerland
   l) Prussia
   m) Spanish Netherlands
   n) Holland

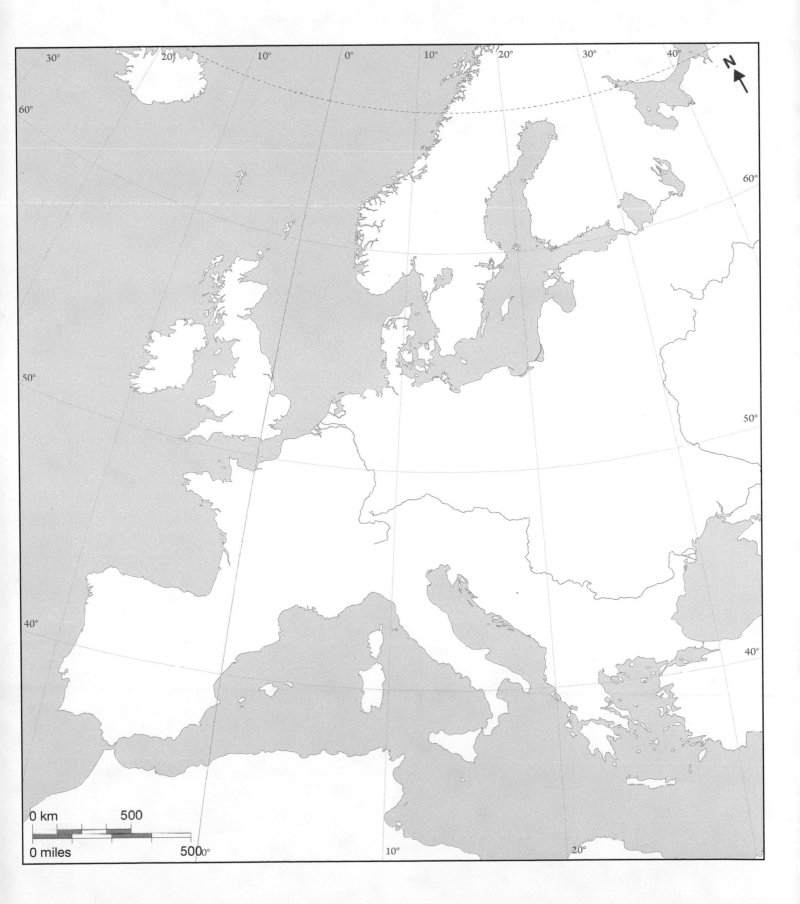

30° 20° 10° 0° 10° 20° 30° 40°

60°

60°

50°

50°

40°

40°

0 km   500

0 miles   500

10° 20°

115